Mary Bowen Liz Hocking

English World

Workbook 6

1 Study skills

Do you remember the abc?

a b c d e f g h i j k l m n o p q r s t u v w x y z

1 (abc) **Write the words in the correct order.**

1	thrilling	dangerous	active	weird	rough
2	spring	fire	island	tap	Iceland
3	erupt	cut	heat	climb	bubble
4	student	rock	power	dragon	pool
5	incredible	rough	brilliant	smooth	sharp
6	melt	freeze	cool	boil	steam

2 Match the words and the definitions.

volcano   guide   shoot   glacier   peculiar   fountain   lava   crater

1 a place where water rises up into the air: _____
2 a kind of mountain: _____
3 a large area of ice which moves down a valley: _____
4 the central part of a volcano: _____
5 very strange, weird: _____
6 a person who shows a place to visitors: _____
7 the liquid rock which flows from a volcano: _____
8 to move very quickly: _____

Now check the words in your Dictionary.

Unit 1 Dictionary skills

Reading comprehension and vocabulary

1 Read *The land of fire and ice* again.

2 Read the sentences. When did these things happen? Write the day.

1 Ari drew a diagram of Hekla. __Monday__
2 Andy and his father swam in a hot spring. _____
3 Andy's father took a picture of a geyser. _____
4 Andy and his father flew over the island. _____
5 Ari, Andy and his father went inside a volcano. _____
6 Ari talked about lava rock. _____
7 Andy heard strange sounds from the mud pots. _____
8 Ari gave Andy a picture of Hekla erupting. _____

3 Match the phrases to the pictures.

1 rough and sharp
2 thrilling and noisy
3 active and dangerous
4 bubbling and hot
5 hot and high
6 huge and warm

a
_____

b
_____

c
_____

d
_____

e
_____

f
_____

Unit 1 Identifying statements; adjectival phrases

Grammar

1 Complete the sentences with the words in the box. Use the present continuous.

> take   leave   go   spend   fly   perform

1 We ___are going___ to the mall tomorrow afternoon.
2 Uncle Joe _____ to America on Sunday.
3 _____ you _____ your exams next week?
4 I _____ not _____ my next holidays in the city.
5 The children _____ their play tomorrow.
6 Our train _____ at three o'clock.

2 Look at Joe's list. Answer the questions.

1 When is he playing football?
_____

2 Who is Joe seeing on Tuesday?
_____

3 What is happening on Saturday morning?
_____

4 When are they having a party?
_____

5 Where are Joe and Bob going on Friday?
_____

Monday at 5 - football match
Saturday morning - Grandma and Grandpa arriving
Birthday party for Mum Saturday evening
Tuesday - dentist, 10 o'clock
Friday - school play with Bob

3 How about you? Write about your plans. Use the present continuous.

1 Tomorrow _____
2 On Friday _____
3 Next week _____
4 At the weekend _____
5 Next year _____

4 Unit 1   Present continuous with future meaning

Grammar in conversation

1 Complete the exclamations with *What*, *What a* or *What an*.

1 _____ beautiful beach!
2 _____ exciting film!
3 _____ lovely music!
4 _____ clever children!
5 _____ interesting photos!
6 _____ old house!
7 _____ freezing water!
8 _____ weird noise!

2 Write an exclamation under each picture. Start with *What*, *What a* or *What an*.

Don't forget the exclamation marks!

1

2

3

4

Unit 1   Exclamations: *What a / an ...! What ...!*

Spelling

Remember!
For most nouns ending with o, we add es to make them plural.

This is a volcano.    Here are two volcanoes.

1 Find and underline the plurals. Circle the picture. Write the word.

1 b g s t o m a t o e s l t a w   _____

2 f u h f h e r o e s t i f v o   _____

3 d l f l a m i n g o e s a s t   _____

4 a s v o l c a n o e s e b r o   _____

5 y a m p o t a t o e s h a b   _____

Remember!
For nouns ending oo, we add s.

Some words ending o do not follow the rules.

2 Match and write the plural word under the correct picture.

| kangaroo   piano   cockatoo   zoo   photo   hippo |

1 _____   2 _____   3 _____

4 _____   5 _____   6 _____

Unit 1   Spelling: words ending o

Use of English — Some nouns name things that you cannot see.

Look at the geyser. What incredible power!

1 Read.

Remember: a noun is a naming word. These nouns name objects:

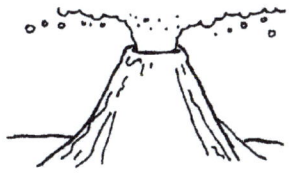   

volcano   geyser   geologist   rock

Proper nouns name people and places.

   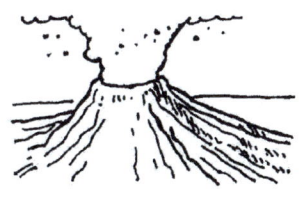

Iceland   Ari   Andy   Hekla

Some nouns name things you cannot see, hear, touch, taste or smell.

You can feel and think these things. They are nouns, too. They are abstract nouns.

> fear   danger   happiness   kindness   anger   beauty   power

2 Match the adjectives and the abstract nouns. Write the words.

frightened	power	1 _____
dangerous	beauty	2 _____
happy	anger	3 _____
kind	fear	4 _frightened fear_
angry	happiness	5 _____
beautiful	danger	6 _____
powerful	kindness	7 _____

Unit 1 Abstract nouns **7**

Writing preparation

1 Read.

On Sunday Andy and his dad visited some different places. Write the words.

> volcano   mud pot   cave   glacier   geyser   waterfall   hot spring

_____   _____   _____   _____

_____   _____   _____

Which places do you think are the most interesting and exciting?

Choose three places. Note them here. _____

How did they travel to the place?

Choose one. Note it here. _____

2 Read.

On Monday Andy and his dad went in a boat. Look at these pictures. Choose which trip they did.

Why did they choose the trip? Write the reason here.

_____

8   Unit 1   Selecting ideas and making notes

Composition practice

1 **Read this word bank. Check any new words in your Dictionary.**

peculiar	noisy	thrilling	funny	dangerous	freezing
boiling	rough	quiet	smooth	warm	cool
weird	terrific	wonderful	gigantic	strange	scary

2 **Write Andy's diary for the next two days.**

What did he see? What was it like? What did he hear? feel? think? do?

Use the pictures on page 8 for ideas. Use your notes and the word bank.

Remember! A diary is written in the first person. Use I and we.

Sunday _____

_____
_____
_____
_____
_____
_____
_____
_____
_____

Unit 1 Diary entries

Check-up 1

1 Complete the sentences with the words in the box.
Use the present continuous.

> give   have   take   play   drive   spend   go   visit

1 They _____ their next holidays in the mountains.
2 Our teacher _____ us a test next week.
3 When _____ the children _____ their grandparents?
4 Jim _____ in a football match on Wednesday.
5 I _____ not _____ to the mall tomorrow.
6 _____ Uncle Fred _____ his old car to the coast?
7 We _____ a picnic tomorrow afternoon.
8 _____ you _____ your exams next month?

2 Answer the questions.

1 What are you doing next week?
_____

2 What are you and your friends doing after school?
_____

3 What is your family doing at the weekend?
_____

3 Complete the exclamations with *What*, *What a* or *What an*.

1 _____ fantastic film!
2 _____ noisy children!
3 _____ amazing photo!
4 _____ delicious juice!
5 _____ interesting holiday!
6 _____ beautiful flowers!
7 _____ heavy rain!
8 _____ difficult exam!

Unit 1   Revision

Check-up 1

4 Look at the notice board.

5 Think about these questions.

1 When is Dad going to France? Is he flying there or taking the train?

   When is he getting home?

2 Who is Billy seeing on Tuesday?

3 Where are Mum and Billy going on Wednesday?

   Why do you think Annie can't go with them?

4 What's Mum doing on Friday?

5 Who is arriving on Saturday morning?

6 What's happening on Saturday evening?

6 Write about the family's busy week.

_____

_____

_____

_____

_____

_____

_____

_____

2 Study skills

1 Read and guess the meaning of the underlined words. Don't look in your Dictionary! Circle your guesses.

Look at these wonderful words!

1 We sat under the <u>magnolia</u> and listened to the bees buzzing in its flowers.
   a an umbrella   b a small plant   c a tree

2 Grandfather picked up the heavy <u>tome</u> from the table and started to read.
   a a box   b a book   c a cloth

3 Small white flowers were growing in the green <u>turf</u> beneath our feet.
   a leaves   b earth   c grass

4 John pushed his feet into the tall red <u>wellies</u> and went out into the rain.
   a boots   b shoes   c gloves

5 Joe put his foot on the <u>accelerator</u> and the car shot forward.
   a it stops a car   b it makes a car go faster   c it plays music

6 The children's faces were <u>flushed</u> with excitement.
   a red   b white   c sad

Did you guess correctly? Ask your teacher!

2 Can you remember the missing words? They were all in the Reading text. Complete the words.

1 The radio isn't working. It needs a new b_____.
2 A large a_____ of snow has fallen on the mountains.
3 Billy, please turn round and f_____ the board.
4 The moon is so bright! Look how it is r_____ on the sea!
5 Be careful! That knife has a very sharp b_____.
6 This island has a very rocky c_____.
7 The Earth has n_____ energy such as wind and water.
8 We can't light a fire. The wood has r_____ o_____.

Now check the words in your Dictionary.

Unit 2   Dictionary skills

Reading comprehension and vocabulary

1 Read *Energy is all around us* again.

2 Read the sentences. Number them in order.

a ___ The turbine turns a generator.

b ___ The liquid at the top of the tower gets very hot.

c _1_ Hundreds of mirrors are arranged around a tall tower.

d ___ The hot liquid is used to make steam.

e ___ The mirrors reflect the sunlight onto the top of the tower.

f ___ The generator makes electricity.

g ___ The steam turns a turbine.

h ___ Sunlight shines onto the mirrors.

3 Read the words.

steam	nature	generator	tide	turbine
energy	wave	calculator	power	

A Find three nouns that name things to do with water.

1 _____ 2 _____ 3 _____

B Find three nouns that name machines.

1 _____ 2 _____ 3 _____

C Find three nouns that name things you cannot see, hear, smell or touch.

1 _____ 2 _____ 3 _____

Unit 2 Ordering sentences; categorising nouns

Grammar

1 Look, read and answer the questions.

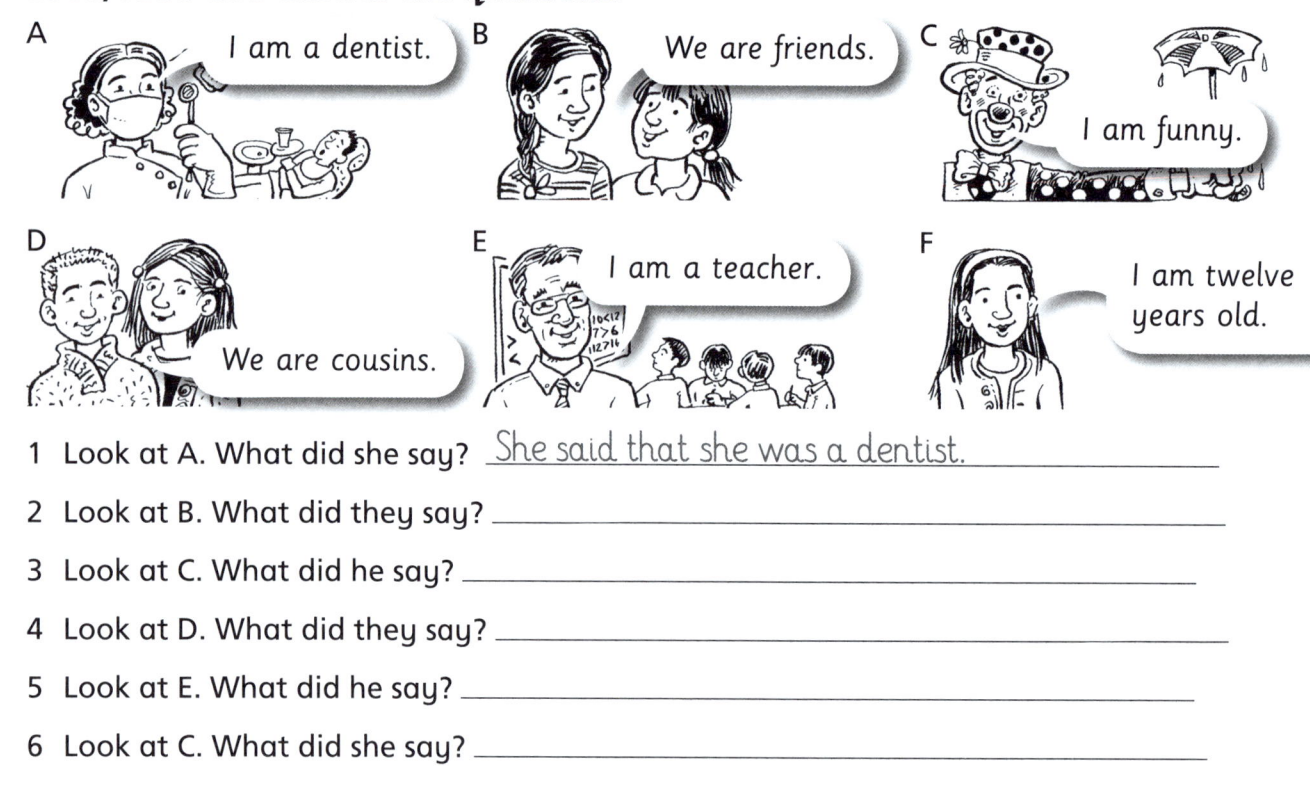

1. Look at A. What did she say? <u>She said that she was a dentist.</u>
2. Look at B. What did they say? _____
3. Look at C. What did he say? _____
4. Look at D. What did they say? _____
5. Look at E. What did he say? _____
6. Look at C. What did she say? _____

2 Read the sentences. Write the speech bubbles.

1. He said that he was a pilot.

2. She said that she was busy.

3. They said that they were eleven.

4. She said that she was a teacher.

5. He said that he was ill.

6. They said that they were sisters.

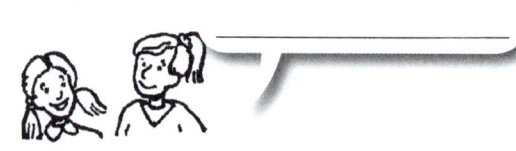

Grammar in conversation

1 Look and read. Write *Yes* or *No*.

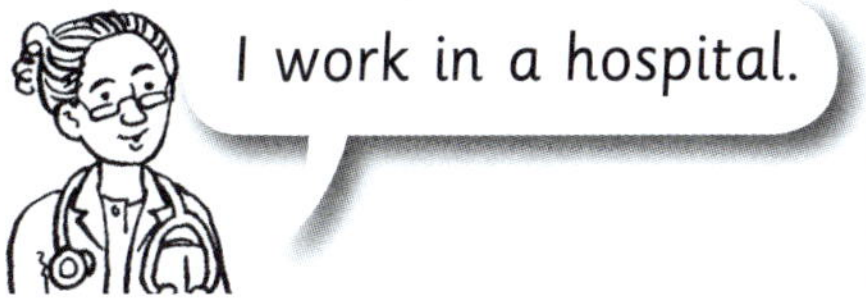

Speech bubbles:
- I work in a hospital.
- I play the piano.
- We go to a good school.
- I can run fast.
- We feel sad.
- I write poems.

1  He said he played the guitar. _____

2  She said she worked in a hospital. _____

3  They said they felt happy. _____

4  They said they went to a good school. _____

5  She said she wrote stories. _____

6  He said he could run fast. _____

Correct the sentences which are wrong.

_____

_____

_____

2 What did they say? Write sentences.

1  I can swim.   He said _____

2  I play football.   _____

3  We have a cat.   _____

4 I make lovely cakes. _____

Unit 2   Reported speech   15

Spelling

Remember! We can divide words into parts. The parts are called syllables. Each syllable has a vowel sound.

---

sea
one-syllable word

river
two-syllable word

---

1 Read these words.

> turbine   coast   tower   Earth   steam   mirror

Write the words in the correct list.

one-syllable words   _____ _____ _____

two-syllable words   _____ _____ _____

2 Write the words. Count the syllables. Write the number.

1   2   3   4   5

___ ☐   ___ ☐   ___ ☐   ___ ☐   ___ ☐

3 Read these words. Circle the one-syllable words.

liquid   power   heat   light

dry   lake   sunny   station   hot

4 Write two sentences. Use a one-syllable word and a two-syllable word from exercise 3.

_____

_____

Unit 2   Spelling: one- and two-syllable words

Use of English  We can add different endings to nouns to make adjectives.

ful | power + ful → powerful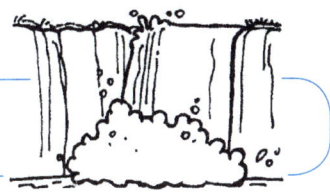

1 Read these words and the ending *ful*. Write the words.

1 care + ful _____   2 help + ful _____

2 colour + ful _____   4 use + ful _____

 Be careful!   beauty + ful → beautiful

less | care + less → careless

2 Read these words and the ending *less*. Write the words.

1 power + less _____

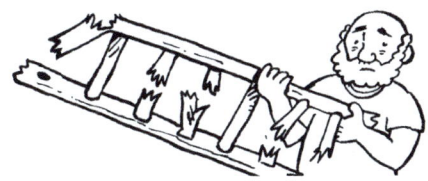

2 use + less _____

3 fear + less _____

4 tooth + less _____

y | hair + y → hairy

3 Read these words and the ending *y*. Write the words.

1 dirt + y _____   2 sand + y _____   3 rock + y _____

 Be careful!   sun + y → sunny   wave + y → wavy

Unit 2 Adding endings to nouns to make adjectives   **17**

Writing preparation

1 Match the words to the objects.

> turbine   generator   battery   wave   power station

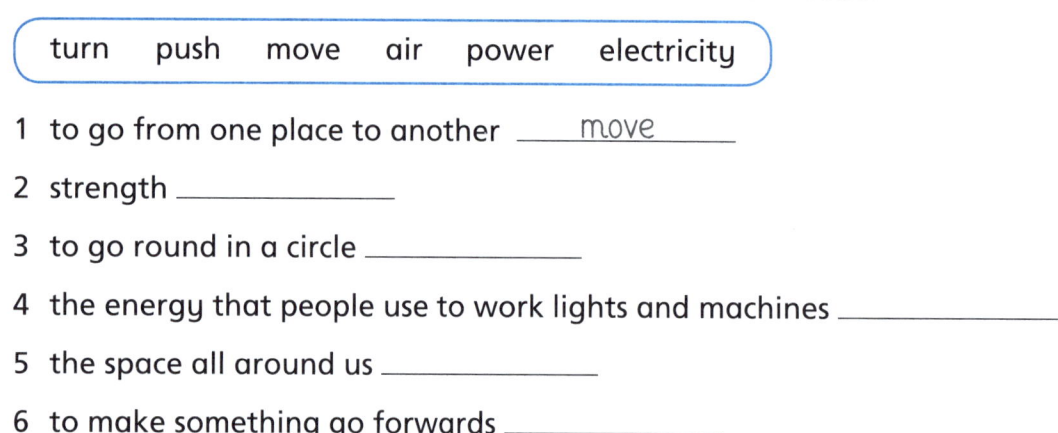

1 _____ 2 _____ 3 _____ 4 _____ 5 _____

2 Match the words and the definitions. Write the words.

> turn   push   move   air   power   electricity

1 to go from one place to another ___move___

2 strength _____

3 to go round in a circle _____

4 the energy that people use to work lights and machines _____

5 the space all around us _____

6 to make something go forwards _____

3 What do you know about the power of the sea and waves? Write notes.

4 Label the diagrams on page 19.

5 Write three paragraphs about wave power on page 19.

1 Write about the power of the sea and waves. Use your notes.

2 Explain how a wave power station works. Use the diagram to help you explain.

3 How is wave power used in Scotland? Use the diagram to help you explain.

Unit 2   Vocabulary

Composition practice

> Remember! When we explain how things work, we use the present tense.

Wave power

A wave power station

This is how the wave power station works:

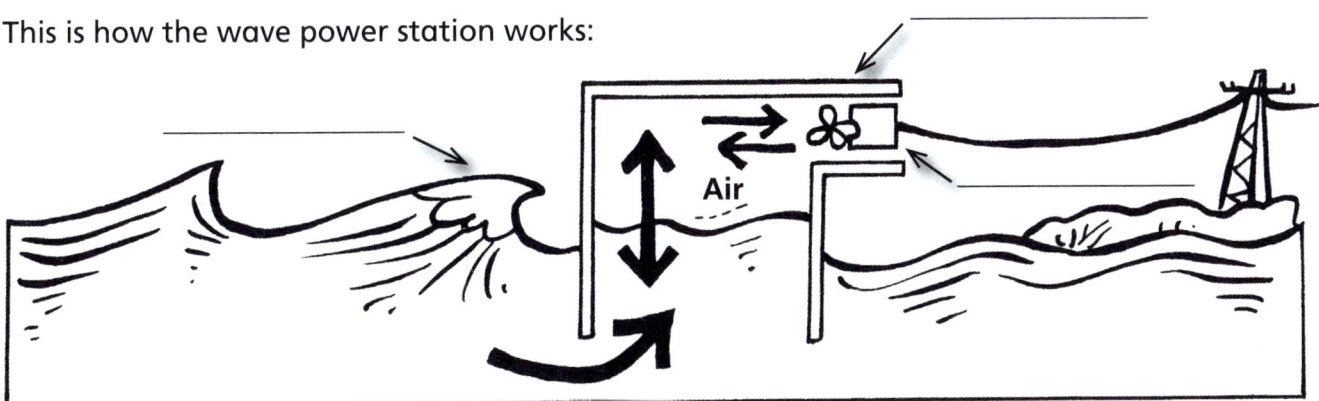

First, the waves

How wave power is used in Scotland

Unit 2   Explanation of a process

Check-up 2

1 What did they say? Write sentences.

1 I'm tired.   He said that _____
2 We're twelve.   _____
3 I'm Russian.   _____
4 We are teachers.   _____
5 I'm hungry.   _____

2 What did they say? Write sentences.

1 "I have two brothers," said the girl.   The girl said _____
2 Joe said, "I can play the piano."   _____
3 "We never go to the beach," said Harry.   _____
4 "I feel ill," the girl said.   _____
5 The man said, "I speak French."   _____
6 The boys said, "We work hard."   _____

3 Read the sentences. Write the speech bubbles.

1

The girl said that she came from America.

2

The man said that he drove a fast car.

3

The boys said they knew how to cook.

4

The girls said that they were sisters.

Unit 2 Revision

Check-up 2

4 Look and read.

Andy and his dad were on holiday in Iceland.

5 Think about these questions.

1 Where did Dad and Andy go for their holiday? What did Andy say on the first day?
2 Was the climb hard or easy? What did Andy say?
3 Did they look into the crater? What did Andy say?
4 Where did they go on the second day? What did Dad say?
5 Was the water warm or cold? What did Andy say?
6 What did Andy and Dad agree?

6 Write about Dad and Andy's holiday in Iceland.

___

___

___

___

___

Unit 2   Revision

3 Study skills

Do you remember these abbreviations?

1 Match.

n   v   adj   adv

verb   adverb   noun   adjective

2 Read and write the correct abbreviations.

1 The sky was cloudy.
2 Lots of people worked at the factory.
3 It looks like an interesting place.
4 They walked beside the river.
5 Come here quickly!
6 Suddenly they heard voices.
7 The voices were getting closer.
8 Yesterday the children went fishing.

cloudy _____
factory _____
interesting _____
walked _____
quickly _____
voices _____
were getting _____
yesterday _____

3 Read and write the correct words.

1 The river doesn't look pretty today.
2 They walked towards the old building.
3 The gate was locked with a heavy padlock.
4 Jack and Mary heard men's voices.

_____ adv
_____ n
_____ adj
_____ v

4 Match the words and the definitions.

local   dye   bank   gap   underneath   imagine

1 the empty space between two things _____
2 in or from a particular area _____
3 to think that something is true when it is not _____
4 under, below _____
5 the land beside a river or stream _____
6 to change the colour of something _____

Now check the words in your Dictionary.

Unit 3 Dictionary skills

Reading comprehension and vocabulary

1 Read *Danger at the old house* again.

2 Read the sentences. Number them in order.

a ___ Jack pulled Mary back against the wall of the house.
b ___ Jack looked upstream.
c ___ Mary walked carefully down to the water's edge.
d ___ Uncle Ted thought for a moment.
e _1_ The stream looked grey and gloomy.
f ___ They set off along the bank.
g ___ They set up their rods and began fishing.
h ___ Jack ran over to her.
i ___ Jack looked at the building through his binoculars.
j ___ Suddenly, she let out a gasp of horror.

3 Read and write the nouns under the correct picture.

> padlock   fence   grid   barbed wire   weed   binoculars

1 _____   2 _____   3 _____   4 _____   5 _____   6 _____

4 Underline the verbs from the story.

flow   bank   peer   bump into   gap   iron   shudder   gasp   binoculars   promise

5 Match the underlined words in excercise 4 with their definitions. Write the words.

1 to take in breath suddenly with a small sound _____
2 to say that you will do something _____
3 to look carefully and slowly at something _____
4 to move freely and smoothly _____
5 to make a small movement of horror _____
6 to meet someone unexpectedly _____

Unit 3   Ordering sentences; matching; definitions

Grammar

Be careful to use the correct past tenses!

1 Complete the sentences with the verbs in brackets.

1 After her visitors _____, Grandma _____ tired.
(go, feel)

2 When the boys _____ their homework, they _____ football.
(finish, play)

3 The passengers _____ off the plane after it _____.
(hurry, land)

4 The children _____ their dinner when they _____ their hands.
(eat, wash)

5 When Jane _____ a big bunch of flowers, she _____ them in a jug.
(pick, put)

6 After the rain _____, the trees _____ in the sunshine.
(stop, glitter)

2 Look at the pictures. Complete the sentences with the verbs in brackets. Use the past simple and the past perfect.

1   (pick, take)

When the farmer _____, he _____.

2  (sing, play)

After Jenny_____, Billy _____.

3   (arrive, ring)

Sam _____ after _____.

Unit 3 Past perfect with *after* and *when*

Don't forget the question marks!

Grammar in conversation

1 **Complete the sentences. Use question tags.**

1 It's a lovely day today, _____
2 That boy is a fast swimmer, _____
3 Those factories are ugly, _____
4 Iceland is a fascinating country, _____
5 We're late for school, _____
6 Anna is an intelligent girl, _____
7 You're good at maths, _____
8 The children are very noisy, _____

2 **Write a sentence about each picture. Use the words in the box.**

isn't he?   isn't she?   isn't it?   aren't they?

1

_____

2

_____

3

_____

4

_____

Unit 3 Question tags

Spelling

Remember! Some words end in *dge*. The letters sound like *j*.

edge — Mary walked carefully down to the water's edge.

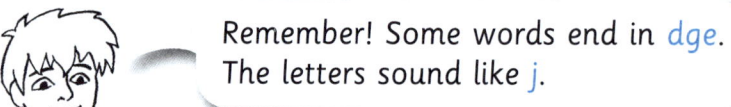

1 Write the words. Read the words.

e → dge → edge
ba → dge → _____
he → dge → _____
splo → dge → _____
fri → dge → _____
bri → dge → _____

2 Answer the questions. Write the word.

1 What can you use to keep food cold? _____
2 What do children sometimes have to show they are in a club? _____
3 What do engineers build across a river? _____
4 What is the word for a thick line of tall plants growing close together? _____
5 What part of a tall cliff must you not go near? _____
6 What is the word for a large splash of liquid on paper or material? _____

Unit 3   Spelling: words ending *dge*

Use of English

Remember! When we write direct speech, we use speech marks.

"We'll be very careful," said Mary.

1 Read.

Speech marks show the exact words that somebody said.

The reporting words can come at the beginning or at the end of the direct speech.

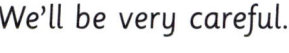
We'll be very careful.

"We'll be very careful," said Mary.
speech marks   comma   speech marks   full stop

Mary said, "We'll be very careful."
comma   speech marks   full stop   speech marks

The reporting words can come between two sentences.

I tell you, Sid. I saw some kids.

Look at the punctuation in these sentences.

"I tell you, Sid," said a voice. "I saw some kids."

2 Write the speech marks for these sentences.

1 It's not so pretty today, said Mary sadly.
2 Jack asked, What's that building?
3 Shh! whispered Jack. Someone's coming.

Do you need help? Look at the examples in exercise 1. Check your work.

3 Write all the punctuation for these sentences.

1 I don't know about that   said Uncle Ted
2 Mary asked   Please can we go and look at the old house
3 All right   said Uncle Ted   But don't go too near

Unit 3   Revision of punctuating direct speech

Writing preparation

1 Read and answer the questions. Make notes.

Uncle Ted and the children went back to the old house at night. Why?

Use these ideas or use your own ideas.

They were looking for something.　　They wanted to watch someone.

They were looking for _____　　They wanted to watch _____

_____　　_____

What was the house like at night?

Was there anybody there?　　　　　　　　Were there any lights?

Think of words to describe the house at night. Write them in the box.

Use your Dictionary.

2 Think about these questions. Choose from these ideas or use your own ideas.

What was the weather like?   cold?   windy?   warm?

What did they see and hear?   people?   a car?   a van?   the stream?   anything else?

Did they find anything?   No ____   Yes ____   What was it? _____

What did Uncle Ted say?   _____

What did Jack and Mary say?   _____

_____

What happened at the end?   _____

Unit 3 Story notes

Composition practice

1 **Write what happened when Uncle Ted, Jack and Mary went back to the old house at night. Write five paragraphs.**

Paragraph 1   Say why they went back.

Paragraph 2   Describe the house at night.

Paragraph 3   Say what the weather was like.
Say what they saw and heard.
Say if they found anything.

Paragraph 4   Write what Uncle Ted said.
Write what Jack and Mary said.

Paragraph 5   Write what happened at the end.

Remember! Use speech marks for direct speech when you write paragraph 4.

If you need more space, continue in your copy book.

Unit 3   Completing a mystery story

Check-up 3

1 Complete the sentences. Use *had* + one of the verbs in the box.
   Be careful to use the correct form of the verb.

   > eat   spend   begin   leave   stop   swim

   1 Grandma felt tired after her guests _____.
   2 When the rain _____, we went for a walk.
   3 The children played on the beach after they _____ in the sea.
   4 When he _____ all the chocolate, Jimmy began to feel ill.
   5 We arrived at Aunt Jane's house after the party _____.
   6 After John _____ all his money at the mall, he wanted to go home.

2 Complete the sentences with the verbs in brackets.
   Be careful to use the correct forms of the verbs.

   1 After the children _____ their homework, they _____ TV.
      (do, watch)
   2 When the boys _____ their hands, they _____ down at the table.
      (wash, sit)
   3 The school _____ very quiet when the children _____ home.
      (be, go)
   4 The grass _____ green again after the rain _____.
      (become, fall)

3 Complete the sentences with question tags. Don't forget the question marks!

   1 Linda's a clever girl, _____
   2 The children are very polite, _____
   3 It's windy today, _____
   4 Tigers are beautiful animals, _____
   5 That man is a famous actor, _____
   6 Our exams are always difficult, _____
   7 That dog is very noisy, _____
   8 These jeans are expensive, _____

Check-up 3

4 **Look and read.**

5 **Read the story and underline the mistakes.**

On Saturday night Danny went swimming with his sister. The weather was terrible. When they had found a bad place to sit on the beach, they started to swim. There were lots of fish in the pond and they caught five. They made a fire and cooked the fish on it. Soon breakfast was ready. The fish tasted awful. After they had eaten the fish, Dad had a sleep under an umbrella and Danny read a magazine. They enjoyed their busy afternoon.

6 **Write the story correctly. Use the words in the box.**

| fishing | lazy | lovely | bank | fish | book | river |
| lunch | good | delicious | tree | father | morning | six |

_____

_____

_____

_____

_____

Unit 3 Revision

4 Study skills

It's often useful to make notes.

1 Read.

The dodo was a large bird which lived on the island of Mauritius in the Indian Ocean. It built its nest on the ground and it could not fly. When men arrived on the island, the dodos were not afraid and did not run away. Men hunted the birds and took their eggs. By the end of the seventeenth century, the dodo was extinct.

2 Look at these notes on the dodo.

```
Dodo – large bird – lived – Mauritius – Indian Ocean
built – nest – ground – could not fly
men arrived – dodos not afraid – not run away
men hunted birds – took eggs
end 17th century – extinct
```

3 Think about it.

1 What sort of words appear in the notes?
2 What sort of words do not appear in the notes?

4 Read about tigers. Write notes.

Tigers live in many countries in Asia. At the start of the twentieth century there were about 100,000 tigers in the world. People hunted tigers for their fur. They also cut down the forests where the tigers lived. Today there are only 2,000 tigers in the wild. Tigers are protected in many countries but they are still in danger.

_____

_____

_____

_____

Unit 4 Making notes

Reading comprehension and vocabulary

1 Read *The bear and the two travellers* again.

2 Read. Choose answer a, b or c to complete each sentence.

1 One of the travellers was

   a careful.   b fearful.   c helpful.

2 The timid traveller froze because

   a he felt cold.   b his friend told him to keep still.

   c he was scared.

3 The timid man could not escape because

   a there was not enough time.   b he was too cold.

   c he could not climb the tree.

4 The traveller held his breath because

   a he was too scared to breathe.   b he wanted the bear to go away.

   c he wanted the bear to think he was dead.

5 The other traveller came down the tree because he wanted to know

   a where the bear was.   b what the bear said.   c where the bear went.

6 The timid man said that the bear's advice was never to travel with a friend who

   a is not brave.   b is scared of danger.   c leaves you when there is danger.

3 Match the verbs and the definitions.

> Check! Use your Dictionary.

| pretend   sniff   repeat   destroy   worry   hide   cry |

1 to use your nose to find out what something smells like _____

2 to go out of sight of everyone _____

3 to think that something bad is going to happen _____

4 to behave as though something is true that is not true _____

5 to call out _____

6 to break and harm something so it cannot be used again _____

7 to say something again _____

Grammar

1 Find the pictures and answer the questions.

1 What did the rider tell the horse to do? _____
2 What did the teacher ask the children to do? _____
3 What did the boy ask his mother to do? _____
4 What did the farmer tell the dog to do? _____

2 Find the pictures and answer the questions.

1 What did the man tell the boy not to do? _____
2 What did the teacher ask the girls not to do? _____
3 What did the woman tell the boy not to do? _____
4 What did the woman ask the girl not to do? _____

3 What did they say? Use *told* or *asked*.

1 "Stand up, everyone," said the teacher. _____
2 "Don't swim in the river, boys," said the man. _____
3 "Please, play quietly, children," said Mum. _____
4 "Don't be late, John," said Dad. _____
5 Lucy said, "Please, don't be angry, Meg." _____
6 "Please, wash the dishes, Tom," said Mum. _____

Grammar in conversation

1 Complete the sentences with the verbs in brackets.
Use the present perfect or the past simple.

1 _____ you ever _____ to China? (be)
2 Freddy _____ to England last year. (go)
3 I _____ never _____ a kangaroo. (see)
4 Milly _____ often _____ by plane. (travel)
5 _____ John _____ to school by bus this morning? (come)
6 On Saturday the girls _____ books and CDs at the mall. (buy)
7 _____ the children ever _____ an orchestra? (hear)
8 The boys _____ not _____ their lunch yesterday. (eat)

2 Complete the questions.

_____ to Canada?

Yes, I have.

When _____ there?

I went there last summer.

What _____?

I saw lakes and mountains.

_____ any bears?

No, I didn't!

3 Complete the answers.

Have you ever eaten Italian food?

Yes, _____.

Where did you eat it?

_____ at an Italian restaurant.

What did you think of it?

_____ it _____ delicious!

Unit 4   Present perfect and past simple

Spelling

Remember! Some words sound the same but are spelled differently. They have different meanings, too.

The bear's paws were huge. Poor man!

1 Read. Write another word that sounds the same but is spelled differently.

1 poor   *paw*   2 right   _____

3 rode   _____   4 wear   _____

5 some   _____   6 past   _____

7 tied   _____   8 wood   _____

2 Complete these sentences.

1 _____ Grandad has a broken leg.

2 _____ is my book?

3 The old house was made of _____.

4 We _____ coats when it is cold.

5 This _____ goes up the hill and through the forest.

6 Is this answer _____ or wrong?

7 We had to _____ a story for our English homework.

8 Does this bus go _____ the station?

9 Can I have _____ water, please?

10 When the _____ comes in, the water covers the rocks.

3 Use these words in sentences of your own.

1 rode _____

2 tied _____

3 passed _____

4 some _____

Unit 4   Spelling: homophones

Use of English

Some words have the same meanings, or nearly the same meanings.

The man was fearful.

The man was frightened.

1 Read. Write the words in the box next to the correct words in the list.

> creature   angry   happy   jump   closed   begin   huge   tiny

1 leap _____   2 joyful _____

3 animal _____   4 enormous _____

5 cross _____   6 shut _____

7 little _____   8 start _____

2 Rewrite the sentences. Use words from exercise 1 to replace the words in blue.

1 We were late and Dad was angry. _____

2 The little bird hopped onto the branch. _____

3 The giant's castle was huge. _____

4 That animal is very strange. _____

3 Complete the paragraph.

Use words from this page. Use each word once only.

In writing, we can use different words for the same idea. This makes writing more interesting.

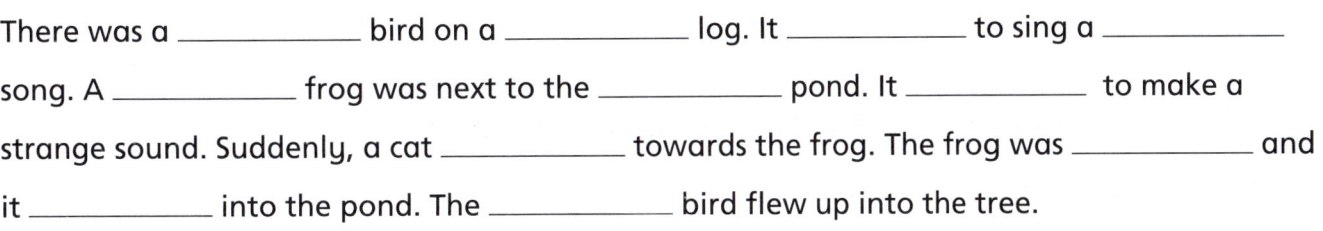

There was a _____ bird on a _____ log. It _____ to sing a _____ song. A _____ frog was next to the _____ pond. It _____ to make a strange sound. Suddenly, a cat _____ towards the frog. The frog was _____ and it _____ into the pond. The _____ bird flew up into the tree.

Unit 4 Synonyms

Writing preparation

1 Look at the pictures. They tell a fable about a hare  and  a tortoise.

Read the words. Talk about the story.

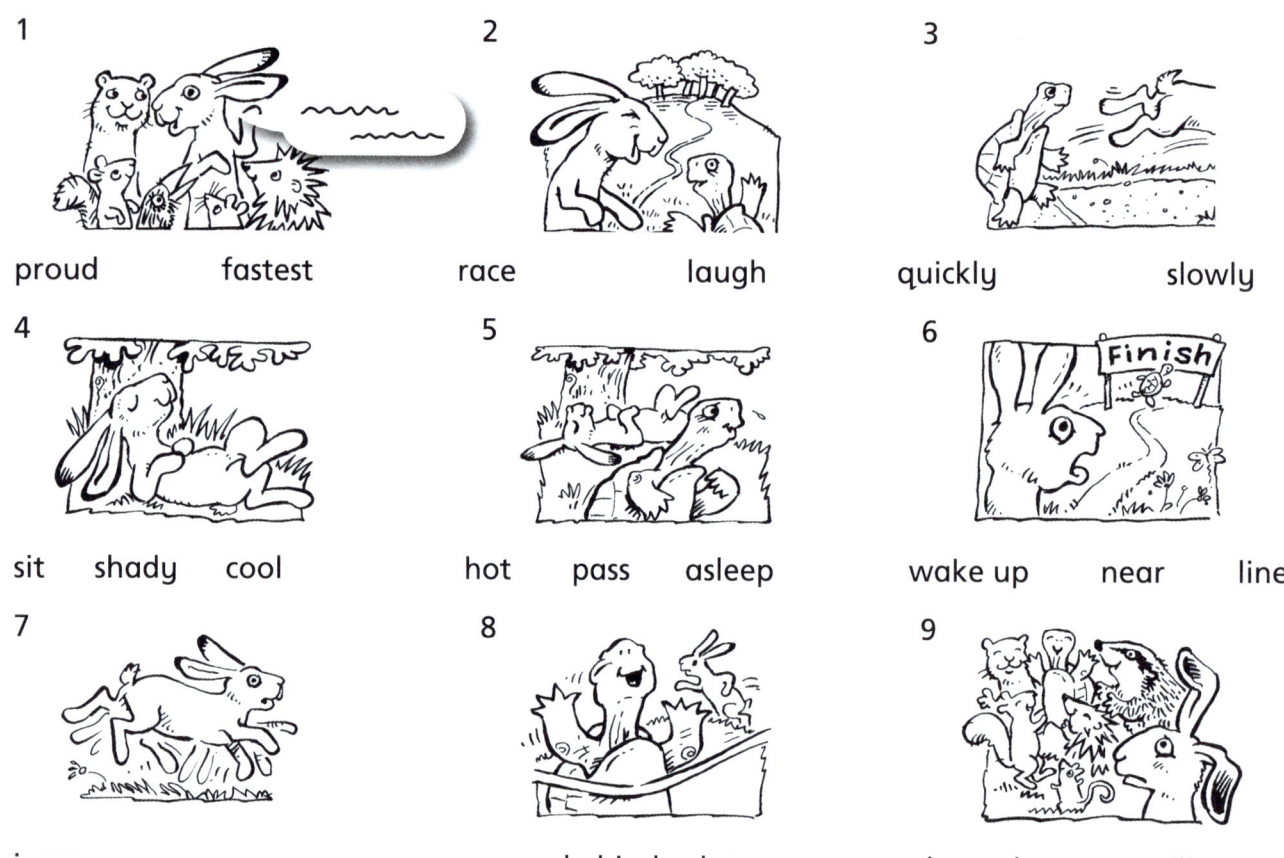

1 proud   fastest
2 race   laugh
3 quickly   slowly
4 sit   shady   cool
5 hot   pass   asleep
6 wake up   near   line
7 jump up   run
8 cross   behind   late
9 clap   happy   silly

2 Think about these questions. Write the speech bubbles.

Picture 1   What did the hare say?   Picture 2   What did the tortoise reply?

Picture 9   What did the animals say?

3 This is the moral. Write the words in the correct order.

Moral: race.   and   steady   wins   Slow   the

Unit 4   Planning

Composition practice

1 Write the fable of *The hare and the tortoise.*

Use the pictures and words on page 38 to help you. Remember to use paragraphs.

Use the speech bubbles in exercise 2. Write direct speech in your story.

Write the moral at the end of the story.

2 When you have finished, read your story. Check it.

Have you used the best words?

Does your writing make sense?

Is the spelling correct? Check in your Dictionary.

Is the punctuation correct? Look on page 27.

Always check your work before you say it is finished!

Check-up 4

1 **What did they say? Use *told* or *asked*.**

1 Be quiet, please, boys.
2 Stop talking, children!
3 Please hurry up, Lucy.
4 Go to bed, Tom!

1 <u>Mr Jones</u> _____
2 <u>The teacher</u> _____
3 <u>Mum</u> _____
4 <u>Dad</u> _____

2 **What did they say? Use *told* or *asked*.**

1 "Please, don't shout, John!" said Mum. _____

2 "Don't be so lazy, Harry!" said Dad. _____

3 Grandpa said, "Don't pick the apples, Danny." _____

4 The teacher said, "Children, please don't run." _____

3 **Complete the conversations. Use the verbs in brackets.**

1 (be, go) _____ you ever _____ to Spain?

　　Yes, _____.

　　When _____ you _____ there?

　　I _____ two years ago.

2 (eat, try) _____ you ever _____ Chinese food?

　　No, I _____ never _____ it.

3 (be, see) _____ Sally ever _____ to the theatre?

　　Yes, _____.

　　What _____ she _____ ?

　　She _____ the Russian ballet.

Unit 4　Revision

Check-up 4

4 Look at the picture and complete the dialogue.
The words in the boxes can help you.
Be careful to use the correct forms of the verbs.

see	a month last summer lots of them Lucky Really Never mind
go	
stay	the weather Australia my mum and dad hot and sunny
be	

Molly: Jack, _____ you ever _____ abroad?

Jack: Yes, _____.

Molly: _____ you! Where _____?

Jack: I _____ to _____.

Molly: _____? When _____ there?

Jack: I _____.

Molly: Who _____ with?

Jack: I _____.

Molly: How long _____ there?

Jack: We _____ for _____.

Molly: What _____ like?

Jack: It _____.

Molly: _____ any kangaroos?

Jack: Yes, _____. We _____.

Molly: I _____ never _____ abroad.

Jack: _____!

Unit 4 Revision 41

5 Study skills

Abbreviations again!

1 Write the abbreviations for these words.

noun _____   verb _____   adjective _____   adverb _____

2 Read and write the correct abbreviations.

1 Matryoshka dolls are made of wood.   wood _____
2 They are hollow.   hollow _____
3 The dolls are beautifully decorated.   beautifully _____
4 Roses mean love and motherhood.   mean _____

3 Read and write the correct words.

1 This pattern represents night and day. _____ v
2 I have always wanted to visit Peru. _____ n
3 The condor is a huge bird. _____ adj
4 It flies gracefully over the mountains. _____ adv

4 Look! Some words have more than one meaning.

1 wave v   I **waved** goodbye to Aunt Jane.
2 wave n   Huge **waves** crashed onto the beach.

5 Find the definitions of the underlined words in the box. Write the numbers.

a The children are laughing. Look at their happy <u>faces</u>. ____
b Please turn round and <u>face</u> me. ____
c It's cold. Shall we <u>light</u> a fire? ____
d I can carry the suitcase. It's very <u>light</u>. ____
e The thieves stole a lot of money from the <u>bank</u>. ____
f We walked along the river <u>bank</u>. ____

1	bank n	the land at the side of a river
2	bank n	a place where people save money
3	face v	to look at something; to turn the face towards something
4	face n	the part of the head with eyes, nose and mouth
5	light adj	not heavy
6	light v	to make something burn

Unit 5 Dictionary skills

Reading comprehension and vocabulary

1 Read *The meanings of patterns* again.

2 Read and complete the sentences.

1 A pattern is a drawing of lines, shapes or objects that is _____.
2 People began to draw _____ thousands of years ago.
3 Many Russian patterns came from _____ life.
4 The painted wooden dolls are in two halves and they are _____.
5 The rose means _____ and motherhood.
6 Some Aran patterns are named after _____ and objects.

3 Look at the pictures. Write the words.

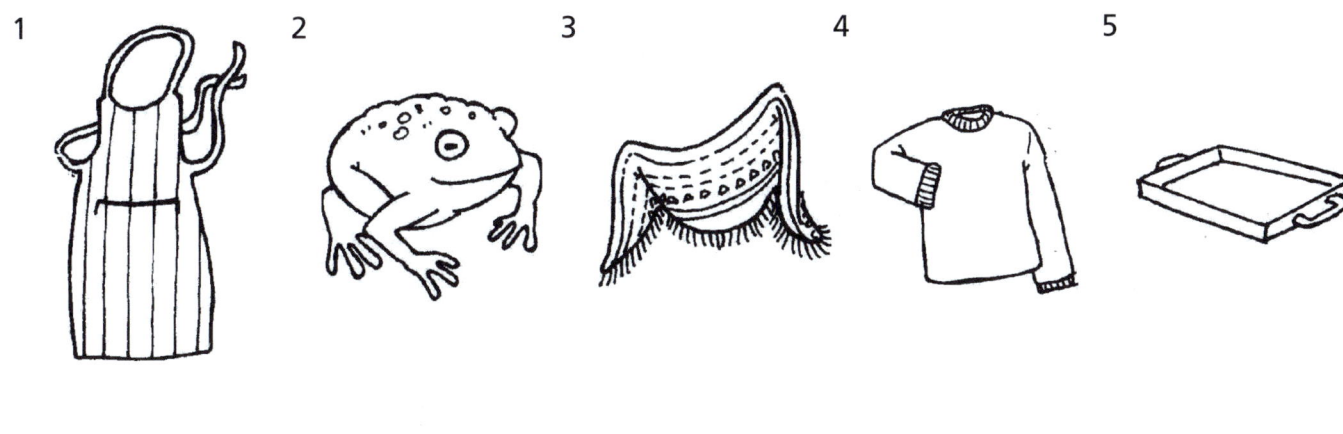

1 _____   2 _____   3 _____   4 _____   5 _____

4 Read the words and the definitions. Write the word next to the correct definition.

> repeat   modern   graceful   ancient   century   traditional   nature   motherhood

1 a period of one hundred years _____
2 the time of being a mother _____
3 very old _____
4 of the present time _____
5 in the way of old customs _____
6 able to move in a beautiful way _____
7 all the plants, animals, land and sea around us _____
8 to do or say again _____

Grammar

1 Complete the sentences with the verbs in brackets.
Use the past simple and the past perfect.

1 The girl _____ the doll that the man _____.   (like, paint)
2 The tourists _____ the shawls that the woman _____. (buy, make)
3 The children _____ the blackberries that their grandmother _____.
                                                                          (eat, pick)
4 We _____ the fish that the fishermen _____.   (cook, catch)
5 The boy _____ the ring that his sister _____.   (find, lose)
6 Meg _____ at the photos that her uncle _____.   (look, take)

2 Look at the pictures. Write sentences using the verbs in brackets.
Use the past simple and *that* + the past perfect.

1   (lose, give)

_____

2   (jump, build)

_____

3   (eat, grow)

_____

Unit 5 Past perfect in relative clauses

Grammar in conversation

1 Complete the conversation. Use the words in the box.

> agree   Well   believe   right   cruel   protect   Really
> mind   opinion   free   disagree   rubbish

Joe: I went to the zoo yesterday.
Milly: _____? I don't like zoos.
Joe: Why not?
Milly: In my _____ zoos are _____ places.
Karen: That's _____! Zoos help to _____ animals.
Milly: _____, to my _____ wild animals should be _____.
Karen: No, no, no. I _____ completely.
Joe: I think Karen's _____, Milly.
Milly: Well, I _____ that animals should live in the wild.
Joe: We'll have to _____ to disagree then.

2 Read. Then write your opinions. Use the phrases in the box.

> In my opinion…   To my mind…   I believe…   I think…

1 Watching television is a waste of time.

_____

2 We should spend all our free time studying.

_____

3 Football is the most exciting sport in the world.

_____

4 Computer games are boring.

_____

Unit 5 Expressing opinions

Spelling

Remember! Some words have silent letters inside them. You cannot hear the letters when you say the words.

often — There are often flowers on the dolls' aprons.

1 Complete the words. Use silent *t* or silent *l*.

ta___k   lis___en   whist___e   pa___m

ca___f   cas___le   ha___f   wa___k

2 Write the words. Underline the silent letters.

1   2   3   4

_____   _____   _____   _____

5   6   7   8

_____   _____   _____   _____

3 Write the silent letters in these words.

i__land   of___en

Write one sentence using these two words.

_____

Unit 5 Spelling: silent letters within words

Use of English

Some patterns have shapes.
Some patterns have objects.

These are simple sentences.

We can join two simple sentences and make one longer sentence.

Some patterns have shapes *and* some patterns have objects.

1 Read.

We can join simple sentences with these words:

and   but   or

There are spots on the plate. There are spots on the bowl.

There are spots on the plate *and* there are spots on the bowl.

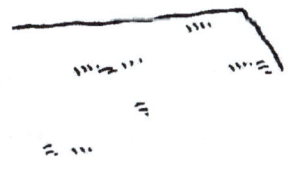 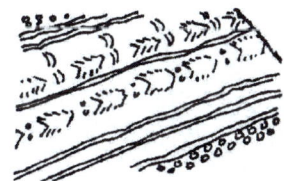

This piece of cloth is plain.   This piece of cloth is patterned.

This piece of cloth is plain *but* this piece of cloth is patterned.

You may choose a blouse.   You may choose a shawl.

You may choose a blouse *or* you may choose a shawl.

2 Talk about how to join these sentences.

1. She can make an apron. She can make a skirt.
2. This shawl is patterned. This shawl is plain.
3. The dolls are in two halves. The dolls are hollow.

Unit 5   Joining simple sentences using conjunctions

Writing preparation

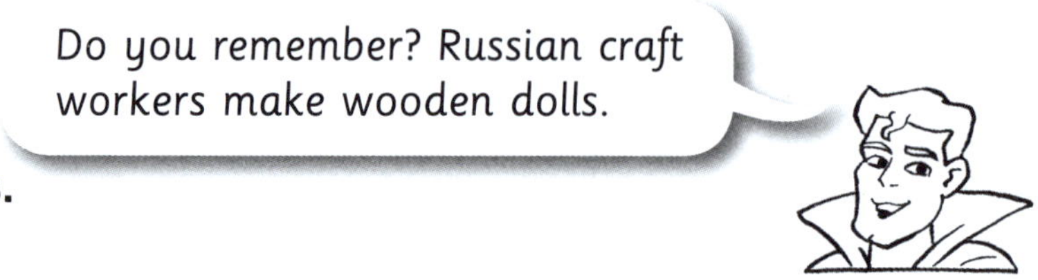

Look at the pictures. Read the notes.

Do you remember? Russian craft workers make wooden dolls.

1. matryoshka dolls – made from forest trees

   work done
   - by machine
   - by hand

   lots of people do the work
   - woodcutters
   - wood turners
   - artists

2. woodcutters
   - bring logs from forest
   - cut to short lengths

   wood turners
   - use machines to turn wood fast – make long, round shapes
   - make doll shapes using machines

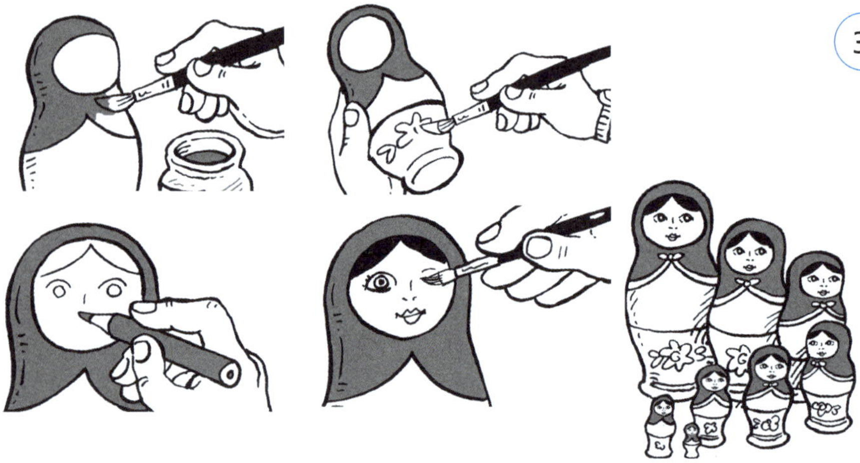

3. artists
   - paint each part of the clothes
   - paint patterns
   - draw face
   - paint face

   usually, all dolls painted with the same patterns

Unit 5 Notes and information for writing

Composition practice

This work is done by people now. Use the present tense.

1 Write information about how matryoshka dolls are made.

Write three paragraphs.

Paragraph 1   Use the notes in box 1 on page 48. Write where the wood comes from, how the work is done and who does the work.

Paragraph 2   Write what the woodcutters and wood turners do.

Paragraph 3   Write what the artists do.

2 Think of a title for your writing.

Think of subheadings for paragraph 2 and paragraph 3.

3 Read your work.

Does it make sense?   Is it interesting?   Is there enough detail?

4 Make any changes or corrections. Read again.

_____

_____

_____

_____

_____

_____

_____

_____

_____

Unit 5   Factual information with subheadings

Check-up 5

1 **Complete the sentences with the verbs in brackets.**
Use the past simple and the past perfect.

1 The old woman _____ the shawl that she _____. (sell, make)

2 Jenny _____ the earrings which she _____ at the market.
(lose, buy)

3 Grandma _____ a cake with the apples that Grandpa _____.
(make, pick)

4 The writer _____ about the place where he _____ as a child.
(write, live)

5 The traveller _____ about the people who he _____ on his journey.
(speak, meet)

6 They _____ the fish which they _____ in the river. (eat, catch)

2 **Read. Then write your opinions. Use the phrases in the box.**

> In my opinion…   To my mind…   I believe…   I think…

1 Eating meat is wrong.

2 Boys are cleverer than girls.

3 Football is the most boring sport in the world.

4 Children should do homework every day.

Unit 5 Revision

Check-up 5

3 Look and read.

4 Read about Billy, Jenny and their family. Underline the mistakes.

What a terrible day! Jenny lost the bracelet that Grandad had made for her. The dog ate the chicken that Mum had cooked for breakfast. Billy found the statue that dad had lost in India. The wind blew down the house that Grandad had built. Mum remembered the cake that she had put in the cupboard. Dad jumped over some boxes that someone had left on the stairs. It really was a wonderful day!

5 Write the story correctly.

6 Study skills

Don't forget your abc!

a b c d e f g h i j k l m n o p q r s t u v w x y z

1 abc **Write the words in the correct order.**

1 Japan   England   Malaysia   Scotland   Russia   India

2 skirt   kimono   jacket   sari   kilt   jeans

3 like   wear   learn   choose   walk   carry

4 interesting   wrong   modern   cool   brilliant   terrible

5 fashion   fluffy   uniform   fantastic   disaster   rehearsal

2 Read and then make notes.

> The children in Miss Pye's class were doing a project about clothes. It was very interesting. First they learned about clothes from around the world. Lucy liked the Indian sari. Joe's favourite was the kimono from Japan. They put on a fashion show, too, and invited their families to watch it.

3 Cover the box in exercise 2 above. Use your notes to write the text.

Don't peep!

Now you can look at the box!

Unit 6 Dictionary skills; making notes

Reading comprehension and vocabulary

1 Read *The most amazing fashion show* again.

2 Match the sentence beginnings and endings.

1 Lucy liked		a	a cotton jacket and skirt.
2 Joe liked		b	a giant ice cream costume.
3 Anna liked		c	a shiny green frog costume.
4 Fred thought that the Scots kilt		d	looked like a skirt.
5 Anna was wearing		e	the sari from India.
6 Joe thought that the kilt		f	was interesting.
7 Lucy held up		g	the script.
8 Joe found		h	a large bag.
9 Miss Pye was holding		i	the kimono from Japan.
10 Mr Barry brought		j	the sarong from Malaysia.

1 ___ 2 ___ 3 ___ 4 ___ 5 ___ 6 ___ 7 ___ 8 ___ 9 ___ 10 ___

3 Write the word next to the correct definition.

> costume   stage directions   lines   scene   plot   character

1 a part of the play _____
2 what happens in the play _____
3 the instructions for the actors _____
4 what an actor wears _____
5 a person in the play _____
6 the words the characters say _____

Unit 6   Matching beginnings/endings; definitions

Grammar

1 Complete the sentences with the verbs in the box. Use the future passive.

> bring   solve   wear   use   put on   invite

1 The fashion show _____ in the school hall.
2 The stage in the hall _____ for the show.
3 The clothes _____ to school by Mrs Barry.
4 The clothes _____ by the pupils in P6.
5 The children's families _____ to the show.
6 All the problems _____ .

2 Make questions. Use the future passive.

1 When – the house – build?
   _____

2 it – finish – soon?
   _____

3 Where – the sheep – take?
   _____

4 they – sell – at the market?
   _____

5 How – the ship – save?
   _____

6 it – break – by the waves?
   _____

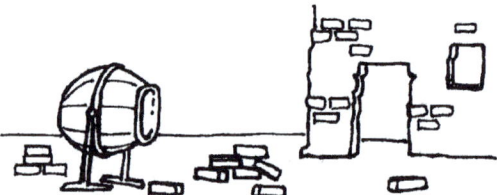

3 Make the sentences negative. Add *not*.

1 The car will be mended.   _____
2 The play will be performed next week.   _____
3 The children will be given presents.   _____
4 The dresses will be made of silk.   _____
5 A hotel will be built near the beach.   _____
6 The school will be shut tomorrow.   _____

Unit 6 Future passive

Grammar in conversation

1 Complete the sentences with the verbs in brackets.
Use the present simple or the present continuous.

1 (work, ride)

This is James Clark. He is a teacher.

He _____ at a school in the city.

He _____ not _____ today.

He is in the country and he _____ a horse.

2 (go, drive)

Lisa and Tom usually _____ to school by bus.

Today they _____ by car.

Their mother _____ them to school.

3 (watch, laugh)

Jim always _____ TV after school.

Today he _____ his favourite programme.

It is funny and he _____.

2 Complete the conversation. Use the words in the box.

| Go away | go on | Why | Well | Tell |
| poem | writing | write | business | |

Katy: What are you writing?
Max: A _____.
Katy: What? You never _____ poems.
Max: _____, I'm _____ a poem today.
Katy: _____?
Max: It's none of your _____.
Katy: _____ me.
Max: No.
Katy: Oh, _____!
Max: No! _____!

Unit 6 Present simple and present continuous

Spelling

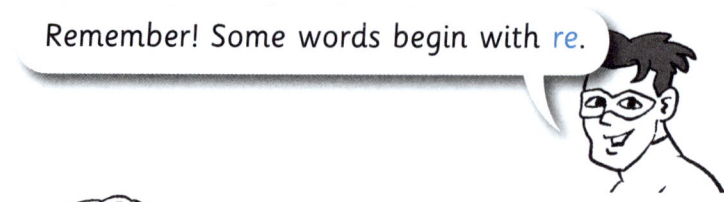

Remember! Some words begin with re.

Ben writes his story.   Ben corrects his mistakes.   Ben rewrites his story.

1 Write the words. Read the words.

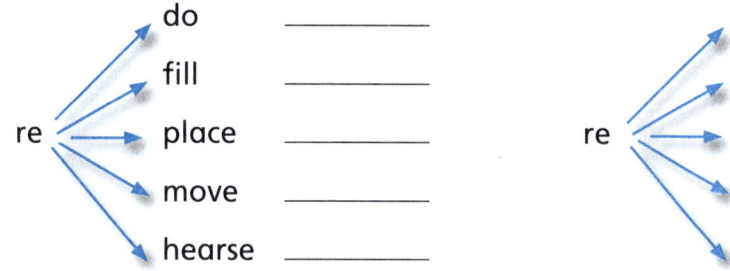

2 Choose the best words from exercise 1 to match these pictures.

_____   _____

_____   _____

3 Choose the best words from exercise 1 to complete these sentences.

1 Miss Pye said, "We are going to _____ the show in the hall."

2 Can you _____ your first day in school?

3 Listen to your teacher and _____ the words carefully.

4 My uncle is on holiday but he will _____ at the weekend.

5 Ben's homework wasn't good enough and he had to _____ it.

6 I like this CD so I am going to _____ it.

56 Unit 6 Spelling: prefix *re*

Use of English

A simple sentence has a subject and a verb.

Miss Pye was talking.
↑ ↑
subject verb

*Remember!
The subject does the action.
The verb is the action.*

1 Read these sentences. Circle the subject. Underline the verb.

1 The children listened.
2 The rehearsal began.
3 Anna was walking.
4 Mr Barry arrived.

A simple sentence can have an object.

Lucy liked the sari.
↑   ↑   ↑
subject verb   object

*Remember!
The object can be a person or a thing. It can be singular or plural.*

2 Read these sentences. Circle the object.

1 Miss Pye watched the children.
2 The children opened the bag.
3 Joe picked up a costume.
4 Miss Pye and the children left the hall.

3 Think of an object to complete these sentences. Write the object.

1 Joe did not like the _____.
2 Miss Pye phoned _____.
3 The wind blew the _____.
4 The children rehearsed the _____.

Unit 6 Word order

Writing preparation

Scene 4 is the fashion show. It's the last scene of the play.

1 Think about these questions. Write notes.

Who has come to watch the show?   the families?   Mr Barry?   Mrs Barry?

Decide which characters are in the scene. Write the names.

You don't have to use all the spaces.

_____   _____   _____

_____   _____   _____

_____   _____   _____

Where does the scene happen?   Write the place. _____

**2 What is each person wearing? Write notes.
What do they say about their clothes? Write sentences.**

Anna is wearing _____

I am wearing _____ . It is made of _____ .

It has got _____ .

Fred is wearing _____

I am wearing _____ . It is made of _____ .

It has got _____ .

Joe is wearing _____

I am wearing _____ . It is made of _____ .

It has got _____ .

Lucy is wearing _____

I am wearing _____ . It is made of _____ .

It has got _____ .

3 What do these people say after the show? Write notes.

the families _____   Miss Pye _____

Mr Barry, Mrs Barry _____   the children _____

Unit 6   Making notes for a play

Composition practice

1 Write the last scene.

Write the names of the characters first. Write the words they say.
Remember to write stage directions to tell the actors what to do.

Scene 4: _____
_____

Write the first stage directions here.

Miss Pye: Welcome to our show everyone. Usually the children

*Don't forget!
Re-read your work.
Make any changes.
Correct your mistakes.*

Unit 6   Writing a scene of a play

Check-up 6

1 Complete the sentences with the verbs in the box. Use the future passive.

> give   build   teach   take

1 A new bridge _____ across the river next year.
2 In the summer exams _____ by all the children in the school.
3 Next year this class _____ science by Professor Jones.
4 At the end of the year prizes _____ to the best students.

2 Make questions. Use the future passive.

1 When – the film – finish?   _____
2 How – the problem – solve?   _____
3 the cows – keep – in the barn?   _____
4 the car – mend?   _____

3 Make the sentences negative. Add *not*.

1 The new mall will be opened in July.   _____
2 The house will be sold.   _____
3 The trees will be cut down.   _____
4 The school will be painted.   _____

4 Complete the sentences with the verbs in brackets.
Use the present simple or the present continuous.

1 (go, drive, walk)

Mr Fox usually _____ to work by car but today he _____ not _____. It is a beautiful day so he _____ to work.

2 (visit, go, study)

Billy and Milly _____ their grandparents every weekend but this weekend they _____ not _____ to see them. They will have an exam tomorrow so today they _____.

3 (sit, enjoy, watch)

Carol _____ in front of the TV. She _____ her favourite programme. She always _____ TV after school.

Unit 6 Revision

Check-up 6

5 Look and read.

6 Think about these questions.

1 What is Tom Park's job? Does he write books or newspaper stories?
2 Where is he standing at the moment?
3 Is the mall open or closed? Are there lots of people outside?
4 When will the mall be opened? Who will it be opened by?
5 Will music be played? Who will it be played by?
6 What will be given to all the children?
7 Is everybody very bored or very excited?

7 Write about Tom Park and the opening of the new mall.

_____
_____
_____
_____
_____
_____
_____

Unit 6 Revision

7 Study skills

Learn to correct your own mistakes!

1 There are mistakes with the verbs in these sentences. The mistakes are underlined. Write the sentences correctly. (v = verb)

1 (v) Lucy <u>is taking</u> the bus to school every day.
_____

2 (v) My brother <u>enjoy</u> playing football.
_____

3 (v) John <u>has gone</u> to Scotland last year.
_____

4 (v) You will see skyscrapers if you <u>will go</u> to New York.
_____

5 (v) Would you mind <u>to open</u> the window?
_____

6 (v) If Sam <u>would work</u> harder, he would pass his exam.
_____

7 (v) The children <u>was playing</u> on the beach.
_____

8 (v) The train <u>will leaving</u> at eight o'clock.
_____

2 Complete the words. They were all in the Reading text.

1 The wind stopped blowing and the sea became c_____ again.
2 The sun was shining and the children jumped into the sp_____ water.
3 In the middle of the island snowy p_____ rose up into the blue sky.
4 Colourful fish and strange sea creatures lived in the coral r_____.
5 We took food, water and a map and set out to ex_____ the island.
6 Behind the trees we found a h_____ cave.
7 Windsurfing and jet-skiing are exciting a_____.
8 The boys could ride well so they travelled through the mountains on h_____.

Now check the spelling in your Dictionary.

Unit 7 Correction techniques; Dictionary skills

Reading comprehension and vocabulary

1 Read *An island in the South Pacific* again.

2 Choose the best word to complete each sentence.

> coral reef   canoe   jet-ski   windsurf   ocean   dolphins

1 Around Tahiti is the clear blue _____.
2 You can _____ across the bays.
3 You can touch the _____ in the bay.
4 You can dive down to the _____.
5 You can _____ round the island.
6 You can _____ across the calm lagoons.

3 Match the words and the definitions.

> attractive   meet   encourage   explore   persuade

1 to say things that help people to do something _____
2 to say things that make people want to do something _____
3 to see and talk with someone _____
4 to go to a new place and see what is there _____
5 looking nice and pretty _____

4 Match and write the words that have the same or similar meanings.

> pretty   persuade   peak   sparkling   unseen   discover   order

1 mountain   _____
2 shining   _____
3 arrange   _____
4 encourage   _____
5 attractive _____
6 explore   _____
7 hidden   _____

Check in your Dictionary!

Unit 7   Cloze; definitions; synonyms

Grammar

1 Complete the sentences with the words in the box.

> me   you   him   her   it   us   you   them

1 John is the winner. Give _____ the prize!
2 The children are bored. Will you read _____ a story?
3 It's Grandma's birthday tomorrow. Let's make _____ a cake!
4 The cat was very hungry so we gave _____ some fish.
5 Are you interested in music? Shall I sing _____ a song?
6 I want to buy a CD. Can you lend _____ some money?
7 We are lost. Can you tell _____ the way to the station, please?
8 I had a wonderful holiday. Shall I show _____ my photos?

2 Change the sentences.

1 I gave the present to her.   *I gave her the present.*
2 I won't sing a song for them.   _____
3 Show your homework to me.   _____
4 We bought a book for him.   _____
5 Dad read a story to us.   _____
6 I've brought these flowers for you.   _____
7 Shall we bake a cake for her?   _____
8 Let's make a house for it!   _____

3 Complete the sentences with a word from each box.

> buy   write   send   play   lend

> me   him   her   us   them

> a rubber   a card   a tune   a letter   a pet

1 Grandma loves hearing from us. Let's _____.
2 They like music. Why don't you _____?
3 I've made a mistake. Please can you _____?
4 We love animals. Mum and Dad should _____.
5 It's Grandpa's birthday next week. Let's _____.

Unit 7   Indirect pronouns: *me, you, him, her, it, us, them*

Grammar in conversation

1 **Read the sentences. Tick (✓) the sentence which is more polite.**

1. A Give me an apple. ____
   B Give me an apple, please. ____
2. A Please, can I borrow your pen? ____
   B Can I borrow your pen? ____
3. A Can I ask you a question? ____
   B Could I ask you a question? ____
4. A Could I have a banana? ____
   B Could I have a banana, please? ____
5. A May I open the window? ____
   B Can I open the window? ____
6. A Could I leave the room? ____
   B May I leave the room? ____
7. A Close the door, please! ____
   B Would you be so kind as to close the door? ____

2 **Number these sentences from 1–5. Start with the least polite.**

A Could I have a sweet? ____
B Give me a sweet, please. ____
C May I have a sweet? ____
D Give me a sweet. ____
E Can I have a sweet? ____

3 **Complete the dialogue with the words in the box.**

| nicely | please | Thanks | Can I | Give |
| sorry | Of course | magic | polite | me |

Jim: _____ me an orange, Mum.
Mum: I'm _____?
Jim: Give _____ an orange.
Mum: That's not very _____. Ask _____.
Jim: _____ have an orange?
Mum: What's the _____ word?
Jim: Can I have an orange, _____?
Mum: _____. Here you are.
Jim: _____, Mum!

Unit 7 Making requests: *Can I…? Could I…? May I…?*

Spelling

Remember! We can divide words into small parts. The parts are called syllables. Each syllable has a vowel sound.

This word has one syllable.

beach

This word has two syllables.

lagoon

Some two-syllable words have a double consonant in the middle.

Explore the hidden pathways.

1 Circle the double consonant in these words.

pa(rr)ot   rabbit   kitten   yellow   apple   hidden
swimmer   runner   coffee   foggy   lesson   pizza

Watch your spelling!

2 Read the clues. Write the words. All the answers have double consonants.

Down

1 weather with fog
2 a round fruit
3 a person who swims
4 not seen
5 a length of time in school
6 an animal with big ears
7 a round, flat food

Across

1 a light colour
2 a baby cat
3 a drink
4 a person who runs
5 a bird that can talk

Use of English

Do you remember? We use **'s** to show the owner of something. An object can have **more than one** owner. Read about the boys.

This is the boys' canoe.

The boys are the owners of the canoe. The canoe belongs to the boys.

1 Read.

If the noun is plural, there is more than one owner.

We add ' after plural nouns ending in s.

birds    the birds' nest

The birds are the owners of the nest.
The nest belongs to the birds.

2 Write the owners of the objects. Write the sentence.

the hens' eggs _____the hens_____   the cows' tails _____
_____The eggs belong to the hens._____   _____

the girls' horse _____   the bears' cave _____
_____   _____

3 Read.

If the plural noun does not end in s, we add 's.

the children    the children's bags

The children are the owners of the bags.
The bags belong to the children.

4 Write the owners. Write the sentence.

the men's boat _____the men_____   the women's shoes _____
_____The boat belongs to the men._____   _____

the people's city _____   the geese's feathers _____
_____   _____

Unit 7 Plural possessive nouns

Writing preparation

1   **Look at the pictures below for a leaflet about a Tahitian boat trip.**

2   **What do the Tahitian people say about boat trips? Write your idea in the speech bubble.**

3   **What can you do on a boat trip? Write your ideas in the box.**

4   **Which activities are the best?**

Choose two pictures. Write captions.
You may write your sentences in
the box.

5   **What can you see on a boat trip? Write your ideas in the box.**

6   **Which creatures are the most interesting or the most beautiful?**

Choose two creatures.

Colour them if you like.

Write captions in the box.

Unit 7   Notes for a persuasive leaflet

Composition practice

1 Write your leaflet. Use you ideas on page 68. Think of a title.

Include the words the man says.

Draw the pictures you have chosen. Write the captions.

Write what you can do on a boat trip. Write what you can see on a boat trip. Set the information out clearly.

2 Look at your leaflet. Does it make the boat trip sound exciting? Is the information clear?   Does it look good?   Make it better if you can.

Unit 7   Writing a persuasive leaflet

Check-up 7

1 Complete the sentences with the words in the box.

1 It's Grandpa's birthday next week. Let's buy _____ a present.
2 The children are bored. Can you read _____ a story?
3 I'll write to you. Please give _____ your address.
4 Nobody wanted this little dog so we gave _____ a home.
5 Are you hungry, boys? Shall I make _____ some sandwiches?
6 We're going to France. Can you teach _____ French?
7 My sister was feeling sad so I told _____ some jokes.
8 Do you like guitar music? Shall I play _____ my favourite tune?

| me |
| you |
| him |
| her |
| it |
| us |
| you |
| them |

2 Change the sentences. Use the words in the box.

1 I bought these flowers for Grandma. _____
2 John played a tune for Grandpa. _____
3 Lily read a story to the children. _____
4 Mum gave my brother and me some sweets. _____

| them |
| her |
| us |
| him |

3 Number the sentences from 1–5. Start with the least polite.

A Can I have some water? ____
B Give me some water. ____
C May I have some water? ____
D Can I have some water, please? ____
E Could I have some water? ____

4 Write questions. Use a different verb each time.

1 You want to borrow your friend's rubber.
_____

2 You'd like to have a sandwich. Ask your Grandma nicely.
_____

3 You need to leave the room. Ask your teacher very politely!
_____

Unit 7 Revision

Check-up 7

5 **Look and read.**

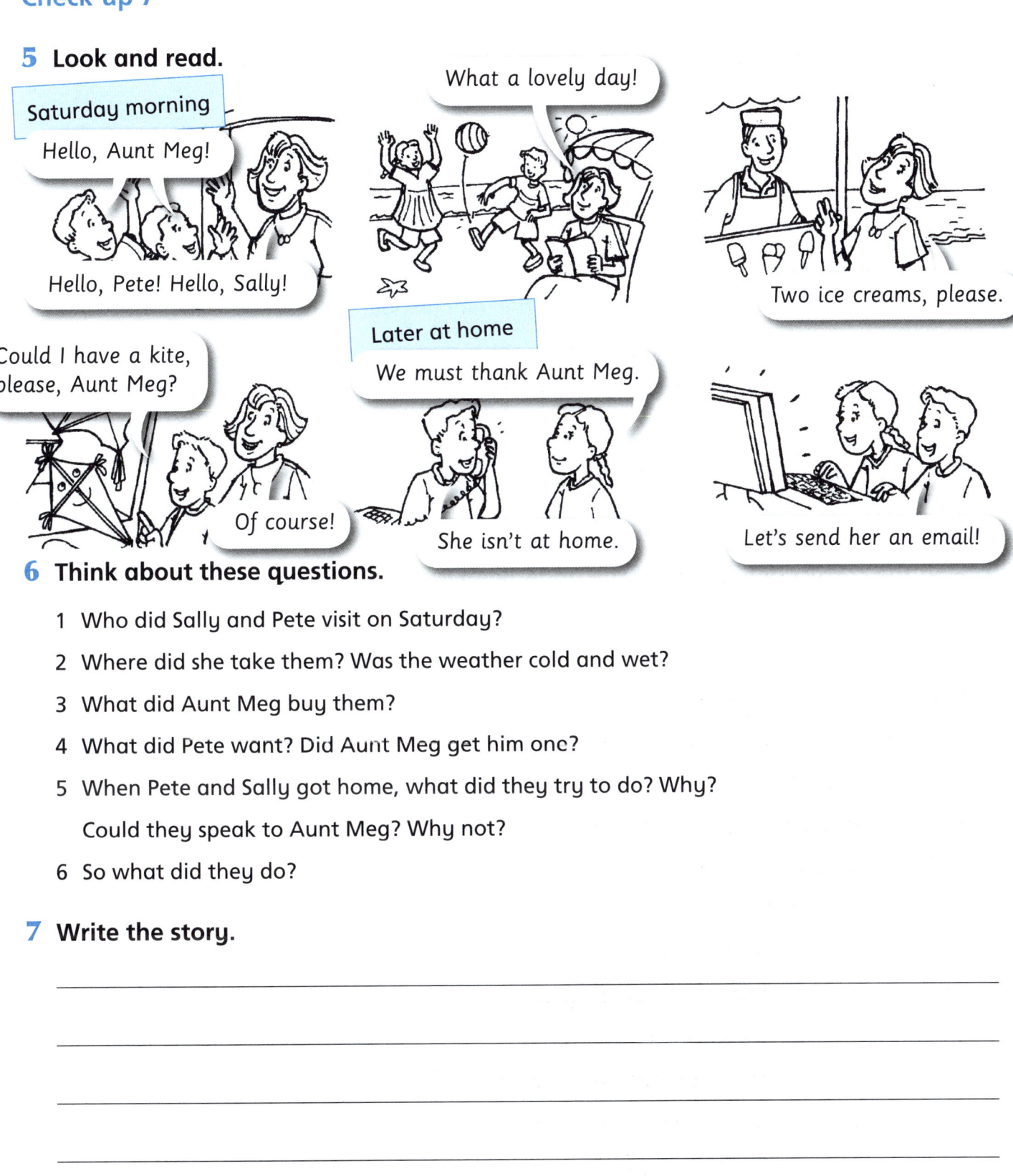

6 **Think about these questions.**

1 Who did Sally and Pete visit on Saturday?
2 Where did she take them? Was the weather cold and wet?
3 What did Aunt Meg buy them?
4 What did Pete want? Did Aunt Meg get him one?
5 When Pete and Sally got home, what did they try to do? Why?
   Could they speak to Aunt Meg? Why not?
6 So what did they do?

7 **Write the story.**

_____

_____

_____

_____

_____

 **Study skills**

Learn to correct your own mistakes!

1 There are mistakes with spelling in these sentences. The mistakes are underlined. Write the sentences correctly. (sp = spelling)

1 (sp) (sp) The children enjoy <u>swiming</u> in the <u>see</u>.
_____

2 (sp) (sp) The <u>acter</u> <u>recieved</u> a prize for his performance in the film.
_____

3 (sp) (sp) Hurry up! The <u>plain</u> is <u>takeing</u> off in half an hour.
_____

4 (sp) (sp) We <u>stoped</u> to look at the <u>ponys</u> in the field.
_____

5 (sp) (sp) The firemen were <u>heros</u>. They saved the <u>lifes</u> of the people in the fire.
_____

2 Find the correct definitions of the underlined words in the box below. Write the numbers.

a The children were <u>longing</u> for the holidays to start. _____
b We watched a very <u>long</u> film. _____
c The elephant picked up the log with its <u>trunk</u>. _____
d The man sat down under the tree and rested his back against its <u>trunk</u>. _____
e The Aztecs were a <u>race</u> of people who lived in South America. _____
f The cars <u>raced</u> round the track. _____
g A black <u>fly</u> landed on the cake. _____
h The birds are <u>flying</u> south for the winter. _____

1	fly	v	to move above the ground using wings
2	fly	n	a small insect with wings
3	long	v	to want something very much
4	long	adj	lasting some time; not short
5	race	v	to move very fast
6	race	n	a group of people who are the same
7	trunk	n	the main, central part of a tree
8	trunk	n	the long nose of an elephant

Unit 8 Correction techniques; Dictionary skills

Reading comprehension and vocabulary

1 Read *How peace came to the people of the great lakes* again.

2 Choose the correct ending to complete each sentence.

1 For many years the tribes had been _____
   a at war.   b arguing.   c fighting.

2 The old woman's daughter had _____
   a a dream.   b a son.   c a daughter.

3 Deganawida paddled a canoe made of _____
   a rock.   b sticks.   c stone.

4 Hiawatha's warriors were afraid of _____
   a the chief of the Onondaga.   b their neighbours.   c Deganawida.

5 The chief of the Onondaga was very _____
   a powerful.   b peaceful.   c fearful.

6 On his journey, Hiawatha fought wild _____
   a beasts.   b bears.   c beans.

7 The chief of the Onondaga had snakes in his _____
   a head.   b hand.   c hair.

8 The tribes agreed to bury their _____
   a axes.   b weapons.   c bows.

3 Match the words with their opposite meanings.

1 peace   a fearful
2 argue   b protect
3 hate   c war
4 sadness   d love
5 ugliness   e beauty
6 brave   f agree
7 harm   g happiness

1 ____ 2 ____ 3 ____ 4 ____ 5 ____ 6 ____ 7 ____

Unit 8   Multiple choice; antonymns

Grammar

1 Complete the sentences with the verbs in the box.
Use the present perfect continuous.

> teach   travel   play   wait   live   learn

1 Mr Jones said, "I _____ in this town for many years."
2 Professor James _____ at the university since 2005.
3 "We _____ French since September," said Joe.
4 Henry and Rupert _____ around the world for nine months.
5 Mrs Bond _____ for a taxi for half an hour.
6 "You _____ basketball for three hours," said the teacher.

2 Write questions for the answers.

1 <u>How long</u> _____

The baby has been sleeping for six hours.

2 _____

The boys have been arguing all afternoon.

3 _____

Aunt Jane has been driving that car for years.

4 _____

We have been watching TV since three o'clock.

3 Complete the sentences with *for* or *since*.

1 Uncle John has been flying planes _____ ten years.
2 The girls have been playing tennis _____ two o'clock.
3 We have been living in our apartment _____ October.
4 Mrs Morris has been working in this school _____ nine months.

4 Answer the questions.

1 How long have you been living in this town? _____
2 How long have you been studying in this school? _____
3 How long have you been learning English? _____

Unit 8 Present perfect continuous

Grammar in conversation

1 What does the boy say to the girl? Use the words in the box.

> So am I.   Neither am I.   So do I.   Neither do I.

1 I'm good at maths. _____
2 I like reading. _____
3 I don't like spiders. _____
4 I'm not feeling well. _____
5 I play the piano. _____
6 I don't speak French. _____
7 I'm going to London. _____
8 I don't eat sweets. _____

2 Complete the dialogue with the words in the box.

Max: What films do you like?
Nina: _____ the "Harry Potter" films.
Max: _____. They're great.
Nina: They're _____ scary sometimes.
Max: No! _____. I think they're exciting.
Nina: I don't like very _____ films.
Max: _____.
Nina: But Harry Potter's _____.
Max: Yes, _____.

> I agree   I disagree   I enjoy
> Me too   Me neither
> brilliant   scary   a bit

3 What's your opinion? Write *I agree* or *I disagree* and one more sentence.

1 It's great to live in a big city. _____
2 Watching TV is a waste of time. _____
3 Every family should have a pet. _____

Unit 8   Agreeing and disagreeing   75

Spelling

 In some words the letter o sounds like u.

son   Her daughter had a son.

1 Write the *o* that sounds like *u* in each word.

m____nth   c__lour   fr____nt   s__n   n__thing

ab__ve   w____nderful   w__n   m__ney   l__ve

Read the words.

2 Write the word with the opposite meaning.

1 back _____   2 below _____

3 daughter _____   4 lost _____

5 awful _____   6 something _____

7 hate _____

3 Complete these statements.

1 There are twelve _____ in a year.

2 There are seven _____ in a rainbow.

4 Which word in exercise 1 is not an answer in exercise 2 or 3?

_____

Write it in a sentence of your own.

_____

5 Solve these clues.

1 The opposite of sister is _____.

2 The opposite of father is _____.

3 This book has a space rocket on the front _____.

Unit 8   Spelling: words with *o* sounding like *u*

Use of English

Remember when to use an apostrophe!

1 Read.

1 We use an apostrophe when we miss out a letter or letters.

Hiawatha couldn't sleep at night.   "I've been dreaming," he said.

    couldn't = could not   I've = I have

Write the apostrophe: I am = I m   we are = we re

                                    he cannot = he can t

2 We use an apostrophe to show the owner of something.

The chief's face was ugly.

    The face belonged to the chief.

When there is one owner, we use 's.

Write the apostrophe: Ben s books   the boy s hand   the bird s wing

3 We use an apostrophe to show more than one owner.

The warriors' weapons were buried in the ground.

    The weapons belonged to the warriors.

If the plural noun ends with s, the apostrophe comes after the s.

Write the apostrophe: the girls bags   the horses tails   the trees branches

4 Remember! Some plurals do not end in *s*.

The people's lives were peaceful at last.

    The lives belonged to the people.

If the plural noun does not end with s, we use 's.

Write the apostrophe: the children s toys   the women s dresses

                                  the men s shoes

Unit 8   Revision of apostrophes of omission and possession

Writing preparation

Deganawida grew up to be a brave, kind and gentle boy.

1 Look at the pictures.
   Decide which pictures show Deganawida was brave, kind or gentle.

2 Write notes under each picture about what Deganawida did.
   Use your Dictionary to help you find words.

Please stop!

Unit 8 Notes for a narrative story

Composition practice

1 Write the story of Deganawida as a boy. Write three paragraphs.

Paragraph 1   Write about the kind things he did.

Paragraph 2   Write about the brave things he did.

Paragraph 3   Write about the gentle things he did.

Begin like this.

Deganawida was a kind boy. One day he

Check-up 8

**1 Complete the sentences with the verbs in the box.
Use the present perfect continuous.**

> play   rain   learn   ride   wait   feel

1 Lisa _____ Russian for two years.
2 The boys _____ football all morning.
3 How long _____ you _____ for a bus?
4 Uncle Fred _____ that old motorbike for years.
5 "I _____ not _____ well recently,"
   said Aunt Jane.
6 What terrible weather! It _____ all day.

2 Complete the sentences with *for* or *since*.

1 Professor Green has been teaching science _____ many years.
2 The children have been watching TV _____ hours.
3 Mr and Mrs Jones have been living in that apartment _____ 1994.
4 Billy has been doing his homework _____ 5 o'clock.
5 Lucy has been speaking on the phone _____ forty-five minutes.
6 Miss Potter has been working at the hospital _____ last July.

3 What does the girl say to the boy? Use the words in the box.

> So am I.   Neither am I.   So do I.   Neither do I.

1 I play the piano.   _____
2 I'm hungry.   _____
3 I don't like exams.   _____
4 I'm feeling tired.   _____
5 I'm not afraid of spiders.   _____
6 I love pizza.   _____

Unit 8 Revision

Check-up 8

4 Look and read.

- Hello, Max. What are you doing here?
- I'm waiting for Joe. We're going to play football. I got here at 9.30.
- It's 10.30 now.
- Yes, and he still hasn't arrived.

- Maybe that's him. Hello? Joe? Where are you?
- I'm at the park. I got here at 9.00. Where are you?
- I'm at the park, too. I'm waiting for you!
- Are you standing by the white gates?
- No! The black gates.
- You said "I'll meet you in front of the white gates."
- Really? Oh! Sorry.

5 Think about these questions.

1 Where is Max? Who is he waiting for? What are they going to do?
2 How long has he been waiting?
3 What happens suddenly? Who is it? Where is he? Who is he waiting for?
4 Is Joe standing in front of the white gates or the black gates? How long has he been standing there?
5 Who has made a mistake, Max or Joe? Has he been waiting in the right place or the wrong place?

6 Write about Max and Joe.

_____
_____
_____
_____

Unit 8 Revision

9 Study skills

Here's a different way to make notes!

1 Read.

We know that the first doctors worked thousands of years ago in the ancient world. In Egypt a doctor called Imhotep treated the pharaoh Zoser. In Greece Hippocrates looked carefully at patients before he started to treat them. In Rome a doctor called Galen did brain and eye operations.

2 Look.

```
                    first doctors
                         |
                    ancient world
                    /    |    \
               Egypt   Greece   Rome
                /       |        \
            Imhotep  Hippocrates  Galen
              /         |           \
        Pharaoh Zoser  looked carefully   brain and
                       at patients        eye operations
```

3 Cover the text in exercise 1 above. Use the notes in exercise 2 to talk about the first doctors.

4 Read.

In Europe two hundred years ago doctors started to use microscopes to look at germs. In Hungary a doctor called Semmelweis realised that it was important for doctors to wash their hands to stop germs from spreading. In London a surgeon called Lister made sure that instruments were cleaned before and after operations.

5 Make notes as in exercise 2 above.

6 Cover the text in exercise 4. Use your notes to talk about doctors in Europe.

Unit 9 Making notes

Reading comprehension and vocabulary

1 Read *The first doctors* again.

2 Complete the sentences with the words in the box.

> illness   microscope   healthy   medicine   operation

1 Imhotep treated _____ 4,700 years ago.

2 Avicenna wrote a book about _____ 1,000 years ago.

3 Doctors in Europe began to use a _____ to look at germs.

4 They did not understand that _____ people could spread germs by touch.

5 Lister said that instruments must be cleaned before and after each _____.

3 Match the pairs. Write the words in the correct list.

> healthy   clean   pain   angry   painful   ill
> illness   cleanliness   health   anger

noun
_____
_____
_____
_____
_____

adjective
_____
_____
_____
_____
_____

4 Complete the sentences with the words in the box.

> fresh   disposable   disgrace   evidence   dressing

1 Harry is in _____ because he hasn't done any homework this week.

2 It is best to eat _____ fruit and vegetables.

3 Mum put a clean _____ on Lucy's cut finger.

4 These dressings are _____ and you only use them once.

5 In our science lesson we looked for _____ that wood floats in water.

Grammar

1 Complete the sentences with the words in the box.

> myself   yourself   himself   herself   itself

1 I hope you enjoy _____ at the party.
2 The monkey is looking at _____ in the mirror.
3 I fell over on the icy road and hurt _____.
4 The boy bought _____ an electric guitar.
5 Aunt Jane cut _____ on a piece of glass.

2 Complete the sentences with the words in the box.

> ourselves   yourselves   themselves

1 "You've done very well," said the teacher. "Give _____ a clap."
2 We passed our exams. We were very pleased with _____.
3 The children opened their eyes and found _____ in a dark forest.

3 Write a sentence about each picture. Use the verbs in brackets.

1 _____ (wash)

2 _____ (look)

3 _____ (enjoy)

4 _____ (hurt)

4 Answer the questions.

1 When were you last angry with yourself?

_____

2 When did you and your friends last enjoy yourselves?

_____

Unit 9 Reflexive pronouns

Grammar in conversation

**1 Complete the sentences with the verbs in brackets.
Use the past continuous and the past simple.**

1 I _____ in the park when I _____ my friend.
(walk, see)

2 Joe _____ across the road when he _____ down.
(run, fall)

3 We _____ a picnic when suddenly it _____ to rain.
(have, begin)

4 The scientist _____ late when he _____ a discovery.
(work, make)

5 Mrs Johns _____ in the mall when she _____ her bag.
(shop, lose)

6 The boys _____ football when they _____ the window.
(play, break)

**2 Look at the pictures and write sentences. Use the verbs under the pictures.
Use the past continuous and the past perfect.**

1 buy   drop   2 climb   start

3 watch   ring   4 swim   see

1 Mrs May _____ when _____
2 _____
3 _____
4 _____

Unit 9   Past continuous and past simple with *when*   85

Spelling

Remember! The parts of a word are called syllables. Each syllable must have one vowel or more.

Say this word! How many syllables can you hear?

ambulance

1 Read the syllables. Write the words. Say the words.

am – bu – lance = ____ _____   hos – pit – al = _____

med – i – cine = _____   im – port – ant = _____

mic – ro – scope = _____   in – struc – tion = _____

How many syllables do these words have? _____

2 Say the words. Write the number of syllables.

1 nurse _____   2 patient _____

3 sheet _____   4 illness _____

5 nowadays _____   6 clean _____

3 Say the words. Circle the words that have three syllables.

germ   carefully   touch   doctor   understand

through   cleanliness   famous   surgeon

4 Write the words from excercise 3 in the correct list.

one syllable   two syllables   three syllables

_____   _____   _____

_____   _____   _____

_____   _____   _____

Unit 9 Spelling: one-, two- and three-syllable words

Use of English

Do you remember?
Some words have more than one meaning.

Florence Nightingale wrote on sheets of paper.

1 Read.

When you look for a word in a dictionary, sometimes there is more than one meaning.

sheet n (1) a large piece of material that is put on a bed

Anna has blue sheets on her bed.

(2) a large piece of paper for writing or drawing on

Use a clean sheet when you copy out your story.

Look back at *The first doctors*. Which meaning of 'sheet' was used in the text?

_____

Sometimes the word can be used as different parts of speech.

treat n a special present or a special event

Dad took us to the theatre as a treat.

v (1) to behave towards someone in a particular way

Grandma always treats us very kindly.

(2) to try to make something or someone better

Doctors treated my aunt in hospital.

1 Look back at *The first doctors*. Was the verb or the noun of 'treat' used? _____

2 What was the meaning of 'treat' in the text? _____

3 Find 'patients' in the text. What part of speech is 'patient'? _____

4 'Patient' can also be used as an adjective. Use a dictionary
   (eg. www.macmillandictionary.com) to find the correct meaning for both forms.

_____

5 Write two sentences using the two meanings of 'patient'.

_____

_____

_____

Unit 9 Homonyms

Writing preparation

1 Name the objects. Check in your Dictionary.

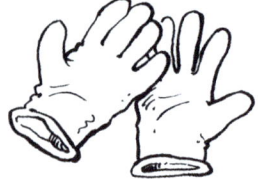   

_____   _____   _____   _____

2 Read the sentences. Underline the sentences that are instructions.

1 You should call an ambulance if it is needed.
2 Do you know where the nearest hospital is?
3 Write your name on your copy book.
4 Do not run in the corridors.
5 You must do your homework at the weekend.
6 This is a really good game!
7 We will leave at four o'clock.
8 Do your work quietly.

3 These people are giving instructions. Write the instruction.

_____   _____

_____   _____

Composition practice

1 **Read.**

If you know what to do when someone is hurt, you can help.

How to treat a burn.

1    2

3    4

Please lie down.

5    6

If possible, …

7    8

Don't worry. The ambulance will arrive soon.

2 **Write the instructions.**

1 _____
2 _____
3 _____
4 _____
5 _____
6 _____
7 _____
8 _____
_____

Check-up 9

1 Complete the sentences with the words in the box.

> myself   yourself   himself   herself   itself
> ourselves   yourselves   themselves

1 Jane made no mistakes in her exam. She was very pleased with _____.
2 Here's some money, children. Go and buy _____ some sweets.
3 Be careful with that knife, Sam! Don't cut _____!
4 The boys fell off their bikes and hurt _____.
5 The man looked at _____ in the mirror.
6 We enjoyed _____ at the party.
7 When I failed my exam, I was very angry with _____.
8 The cat is washing _____ in the sunshine.

2 Complete the sentences. Use words and phrases from exercise 1.

1 Those scissors are sharp. Don't _____.
2 Grandma and Grandpa are going on holiday. I hope _____.
3 Why _____ Annie _____ in the mirror?
4 When the boys didn't win their match, they were _____.

3 Complete the sentences with the verbs in brackets.
Use the past continuous and the past simple.

1 I _____ when the telephone _____. (sleep, ring)
2 Eddie _____ to school when it _____ to rain. (walk, begin)
3 The boys _____ the door when they _____ a noise. (open, hear)
4 We _____ the old bridge when it _____. (cross, break)
5 The man _____ the mountain when he _____. (climb, fall)
6 Mrs Day _____ when a thief _____ her bag. (shop, steal)

Unit 9   Revision

Check-up 9

4 Look and read.

5 Think about these questions.

1 Was Tommy playing in a basketball match or a football match?
2 What was he doing when he fell over?
3 Did he hurt himself? Were his clothes very clean or very dirty?
4 Was Tommy pleased with himself or angry with himself? Why?
5 What did the referee tell Tommy after the match?
6 Was Tommy very angry with himself or very pleased with himself?

6 Write the story.

_____
_____
_____
_____
_____
_____
_____

10 Study skills

Learn to correct your own mistakes!

1 There are mistakes with word order in these sentences. Write the sentences correctly. (w o = word order)

1 (w o) John plays football always at the weekend.
   _____

2 (w o) Never they have travelled by plane.
   _____

3 (w o) At the beach we arrived in the afternoon.
   _____

4 (w o) Why the children are making such a noise?
   _____

5 (w o) The teacher told the children to not shout.
   _____

6 (w o) You don't like bananas and neither I do.
   _____

2 Match the words and the definitions.

> medicines   bones   sore   habitat   blood   pain   anxious   throat

1 the place where a plant or animal lives   _____
2 worried   _____
3 the red liquid that flows though our bodies   _____
4 the part of the body behind the mouth inside the neck   _____
5 we use these to treat illnesses   _____
6 hurting   _____
7 the strong, hard parts of the body   _____
8 the feeling in the body when something hurts   _____

Now check the words in your Dictionary.

Unit 10 Correction techniques; Dictionary skills

Reading comprehension and vocabulary

1 Read *Plants in medicine* again.

2 Label the parts of the plant.

> stem   leaf
> root   seed
> bud   petal
> flower

3 Number the sentences and pictures in order. Try not to look in your book again.

_____ The stem grows longer and stronger.

_____ The petals unfold and the flower opens.

_____ One shoot grows up and one shoot goes down.

_____ The seeds form in the flower and the flower dies.

_____ The seed cracks open and tiny shoots appear.

_____ A bud begins to develop on the stem.

_____ The seeds drop down on the earth.

_____ The seed lies on the earth.

_____ The first leaves appear and the roots grow.

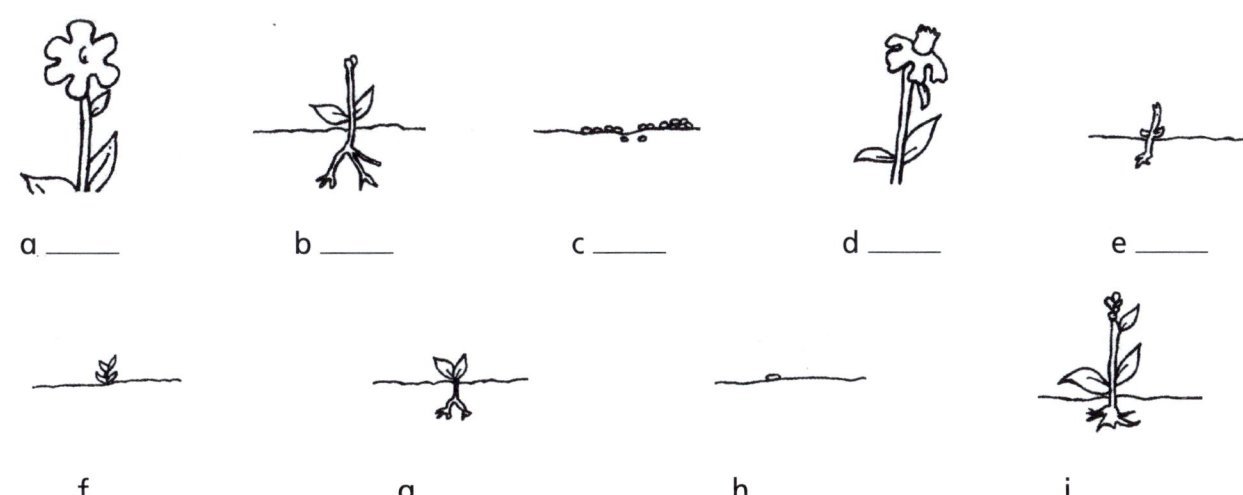

a _____   b _____   c _____   d _____   e _____

f _____   g _____   h _____   i _____

Unit 10   Labelling; ordering sentences and pictures

Grammar

1 Look at the pictures and answer the questions. Use the verbs in the box.

> cut down   pick   steal   break   burn   eat

1. What has happened to the windows? <u>They have been broken.</u>
2. What has happened to the tree? _____
3. What has happened to the cakes? _____
4. What has happened to the statue? _____
5. What has happened to our dinner? _____
6. What has happened to the apples? _____

2 Write questions for the answers.

1. How many _____
   Fifty houses have been built.
2. _____
   No, the car has not been mended yet.
3. How _____
   This medicine has been used to treat fevers.
4. Where _____
   The plants have been found in the rainforest.
5. _____
   Yes, the patients have been cured by the doctor.
6. _____
   Yes, this child has been seen by the nurse.

3 What changes have been made in your town recently? Write three sentences.

1. _____
2. _____
3. _____

Unit 10 Present perfect passive

Grammar in conversation

1 Complete the sentences with the verbs in brackets.

1 I wish I _____ play the piano. (can)

2 Susie wishes she _____ famous. (be)

3 Fred wishes he _____ not _____ a test today. (have)

4 The children wish they _____ near the beach. (live)

5 They wish they _____ on holiday. (be)

6 Do you wish you _____ a pet? (have)

2 Read the speech bubbles. Write about Amy and Jack. What do they wish?

I'm twelve but I want to be sixteen.

I have short hair. I don't like it. Long hair is better.

I love kittens but Mum says I can't have one.

1 Amy wishes _____

2 _____

3 _____

I try and try but I can't whistle.

I don't like being so short.

We live in an apartment. I don't like it.

1 Jack _____

2 _____

3 _____

3 What about you? Write three wishes. Use the verbs can, have and be.

1 I wish I _____

2 _____

3 _____

Unit 10 *I wish* + past tense

Spelling

Remember! Some words begin with al.
Some words end with al.

There are always nurses at the hospital.

1 Write the words. Read the words.

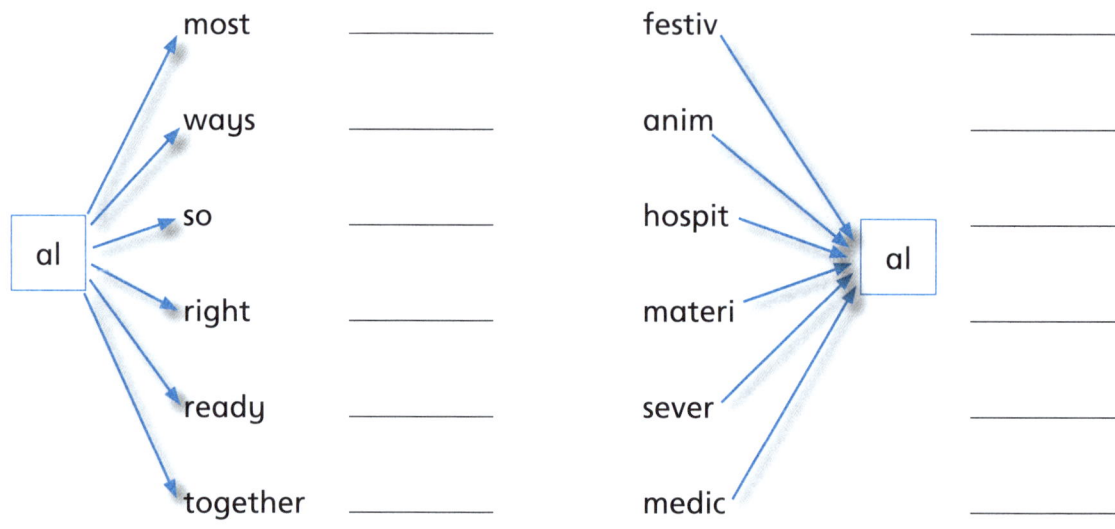

2 Write the words starting with *al* in exercise 1 with the same or similar meanings.

1 safe and well _____   2 nearly _____

3 at all times _____   4 as well _____

5 in a group _____   6 before the time _____

3 Write the words ending *al* in exercise 1 next to the correct definition.

1 a place where sick people are treated _____

2 a living creature _____

3 a time when people come together for a special occasion _____

4 to do with medicine _____

5 a few of something _____

6 something like plastic or wood that can be used to make things _____

Unit 10 Spelling: words beginning and ending with *al*

Use of English

Sometimes in speaking we add extra words to a sentence.

I think rainforests are important, don't you?

Anna, what do you know about rainforests?

We use a comma to separate the extra words from the main sentence.

1 Read.

The extra words can be at the beginning of the sentence.

Sorry, could you say your name again?   Lucy, is that you?

Circle the comma in these sentences.

2 Write the comma in these sentences. The extra word or words are at the beginning.

Oh dear   I've broken my pen.
Thanks   you're very kind.

Well   you can borrow mine.
Alright   just give it back tomorrow.

3 Read.

The extra words can be at the end of the sentence.

I can't hear you, you know. You'll have to speak louder, Anna.

Circle the comma in these sentences.

4 Write the comma in these sentences. The extra word or words are at the end.

This is a good game   isn't it?
No I don't   sorry.

What's the score   do you know?
I'll ask someone else   I think.

5 Write the commas in these sentences. Decide whether the extra words are at the beginning or at the end.

Oh no   I haven't done my homework.
I'm glad you told me that   Ben.

It's Saturday   remember!
Now we can go back to sleep   can't we?

Unit 10 Comma before or after a sentence tag   **97**

Writing preparation

1 Read.

This insect comes from the rainforest. It finds food there. It looks for a good place to lay its eggs among the leaves and branches.

2 Read and match.

a    b   c    d

1 The egg is small and white. _____

2 The butterfly has wings. _____

3 The caterpillar is patterned.

  It has tiny feet. _____

4 The pupa has a hard shell.

  It is often brown or black. _____

3 Read these verbs. Match them to the pictures.

| lays   hatches   eats   sticks itself   breaks open   comes out |

1 _____   2 _____

3 _____   4 _____

5 _____   6 _____

Unit 10 Vocabulary for describing a natural process

Composition practice

1 These pictures show how a butterfly grows. Look and write sentences.
  Use page 98 to help you.

2 Check your work. Think of a title.

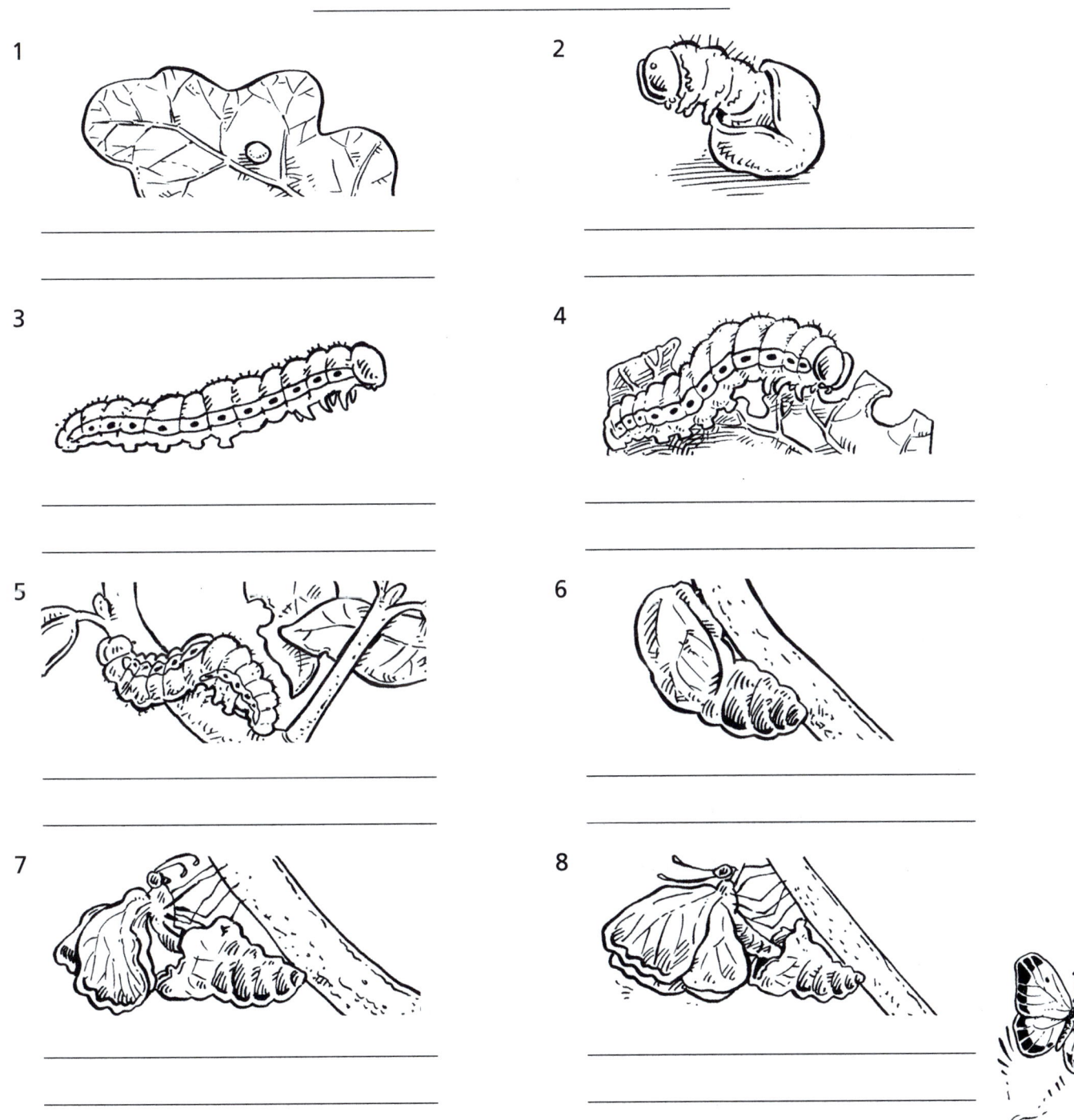

Unit 10 Describing a natural process

Check-up 10

1 Change the sentences. Use the passive.

1 Someone has picked all the flowers.
   All the flowers _____

2 People have heard wolves in these mountains.
   _____

3 An excellent team has won the competition.
   _____ by _____

4 A group of Australian explorers have found unusual animals in this forest.
   _____

2 What has happened? Complete the sentences. Use the present perfect passive. Use the verbs in brackets.

1 (blow down) The tree _____

2 (break) The windows _____

3 (mend) The jeans _____

4 (steal) The picture _____

3 Write sentences using *wish*.

1 Jenny hasn't got a pet but she wants one. She wishes _____
2 Billy can't whistle. He's trying to learn. _____
3 Ann and Jane don't like their brown hair. _____
4 I'd like to live in a big house. _____
5 Freddy wants to be taller. _____
6 We'd like to be on holiday. _____

Check-up 10

4 Look and read.

Ellie and Mike live with their mum and dad in a small apartment in the centre of the city. The city is noisy and busy. Ellie and Mike don't like living there.

I'd like to live on a farm. If I lived on a farm, I could have a pony.

The street is full of cars. I can't play outside with my friends. It's too dangerous.

My bedroom is very small. I'd like it to be bigger.

We don't have a garden so I haven't got any pets. If we had a garden, I could have a dog. I like dogs.

5 Think about these questions.

1 Where do Ellie and Mike live? Do they like living there?
2 What's their street like? Can Mike play outside? What does he wish?
3 Has Mike got a pet? What does he wish?
4 Is Ellie's bedroom big or small? What does she wish?
5 Do they live on a farm? What does Ellie wish?
6 Has Ellie got a pet? What does she wish?

6 Write about Ellie and Mike.

_____
_____
_____
_____
_____
_____

Unit 10 Revision

11 Study skills

Learn to correct your own mistakes!

1 There are mistakes with articles in these sentences.
Write the sentences correctly. (a = article)

1 (a) The name of the great river in South America is Amazon.

2 (a) The highest mountain in the world is the Everest.

3 (a) Animals cannot live without the water.

4 (a) (a) (a) (a) There is plane and helicopter in the sky. Plane is fast. Helicopter is slow.

5 (a) Help! There's a spider in the bath. I'm frightened of the spiders.

6 (a) (a) Is there a easy way to learn words of this song?

2 Look again at page 82.

Let's make notes!

3 Read.

Kitesurfing and skateboarding are extreme sports. In kitesurfing you have a kite tied to your back and you stand on a small board. The wind blows the kite and this pulls you across the water. In skateboarding you can skate on ramps, steps and rails. A skateboarder should wear a helmet, knee pads and elbow pads. A kitesurfer does not need so many protective clothes but it is a good idea to wear a lifejacket.

4 Make notes.

5 Cover the text in exercise 3 above. Use your notes to talk about the two sports.

Unit 11   Correction techniques; making notes

Reading comprehension and vocabulary

1 Read *Extreme sports!* again.

2 Answer the questions.

1 What four main places are used for these sports?

_____ _____ _____ _____

2 What two things are important in extreme sports?

_____ _____

3 What two parts of the body do bikers and boarders protect with pads?

_____ _____

4 Which four sports are not in the Olympics?

_____ _____ _____ _____

3 Read the words. Label the protective clothing. Label the equipment.

kneepads   goggles   helmet   lifejacket   elbow pads

1  2  3  4  5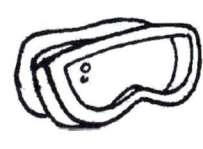

_____ _____ _____ _____ _____

skateboard   canoe   paddles   poles   kite   skis

6 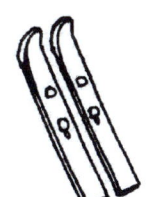 7  8  9  10  11

_____ _____ _____ _____ _____ _____

4 Write the words in the text with the opposite meanings to these words.

1 dangerous _____   2 calm _____

3 boring   _____   4 same _____

5 usual   _____   6 loser _____

Unit 11   Literal questions; matching; antonyms

Grammar

1 Complete the sentences with the correct word in brackets.

1. Summer is the time _____ people go on holiday. (where / when)
2. A downhill skier is a person _____ enjoys skiing fast. (which / who)
3. Trainers are shoes _____ people wear for sport. (that / who)
4. Ski jumping is a sport _____ can be dangerous. (where / which)
5. This is the playground _____ the skateboarders practise. (where / that)
6. In ski jumping the winner is the person _____ jumps the furthest. (which / that)

**2 Change the sentences. Use the relative clauses in the box.
Make sure you put the clauses in the correct place.**

> that downhill skiers wear   when snowboarding became an Olympic sport
> who won the marathon   which the champion rode   where the boys are canoeing

1. The man is from Spain.
   <u>The man who won the marathon is from Spain.</u>
2. The river is dangerous.
   _____
3. I can't remember the year.
   _____
4. Jimmy has bought one of those helmets.
   _____
5. The bike was black and gold.
   _____

3 Write your own sentences. Use the words in brackets.

1. (someone that) _____
2. (something that) _____
3. (a/the place where) _____
4. (a/the time when) _____

Unit 11 Relative clauses with *who, which, that, when* and *where*

Grammar in conversation

Don't forget to use question marks.

1 Complete the sentences. Use question tags.

1 You play computer games, _____
2 The children go to school by bus, _____
3 Your uncle drives a fast car, _____
4 I work hard, _____
5 Anna plays the piano beautifully, _____
6 We all enjoy birthday parties, _____
7 The ski jump looks dangerous, _____
8 You like ice cream, _____
9 Your grandparents live in Australia, _____
10 Harry speaks Chinese, _____

2 Write a sentence about each picture. Use words from each box.

| live   wear   play   enjoy | doesn't he?   doesn't she?   doesn't it?   don't they? |

1

_____

2

_____

3

_____

4

_____

Unit 11   Question tags

Spelling

Remember! Some words for people end in *or*. They are usually people who do something.

competitor

A competit**or** in skateboarding always wears a helmet.

1 Complete the words. Write *or*. Read the words.

act____   doct____   auth____   sail____   profess____

invent____   visit____   may____   tail____   edit____

2 Read the clues. Complete the crossword.

Down

1 This person works on ships and boats.
2 There are thousands of these at the Olympics.
3 You will see this person in a hospital.
4 This person has ideas about making new things.

Across

1 This person watches sports and other events.
2 This person is the leader of the people in a town or a city.
3 This person comes to see you.
4 This person can make you a new jacket.
5 You will see this person in a play or a film.
6 This person checks writing and corrects mistakes.
7 If you go to a university, this person may teach you.

3 Find the word.

One word from exercise 1 is not in the crossword. What is it? _____

What does this person do? _____

Unit 11   Spelling: words ending *or*

Use of English

Do you remember? We can join two simple sentences to make a longer sentence.

The biker rode up the ramp. He jumped in the air.

The biker rode up the ramp and he jumped in the air.

1 Read.

1. Read the sentence again. Circle the subject. Underline the verb.

   The biker rode up the ramp.

   Now do the same with this sentence.

   He jumped in the air.

2. A simple sentence can also be called a main clause.

   When we join two simple sentences we have one sentence with two main clauses.

           main clause 1   main clause 2

   <u>The biker rode up the ramp</u> and <u>he jumped in the air</u>.

   Each main clause has a subject and a verb. What are they?

   main clause 1 subject _____   main clause 2 subject _____

                  verb _____   verb _____

3. Sometimes we can leave out the subject of main clause 2. Read the new sentence.

   The biker rode up the ramp and he jumped in the air.

   The biker rode up the ramp and jumped in the air.

   Does it still make sense?

2 Read the sentences. Underline the main clauses.

1. The children went to the river and they watched the canoes.
2. The canoe spun around but it did not turn over.
3. The woman stood in the snow and she watched the skiers.
4. The skier jumped high into the air but he landed safely.

3 Cross out the subject of the second main clause. Read the sentences again. Check that they still make sense.

Unit 11 Compound sentences; omission of subject in second clause

Writing preparation

1 **Match the pictures with the extreme sports. Write the letter.**

a   b   c   d   e   f   g   h

1 marathon _____   2 canoe slalom _____   3 skateboarding _____   4 wakeboarding _____
5 BMX biking _____   6 kite surfing _____   7 in-line skating _____   8 mountain biking _____

2 **Read the description and complete the chart.**

Extreme sports: The summer games

On the first day the sport was in-line skating and 4,000 people watched it.

The next day was much hotter, 35 degrees and it was sunny all day. On the day after that it rained and 3,500 people watched the kite surfing. On the fourth day it was cloudy but it didn't rain. The competition on that day was skateboarding. On the fifth day it was 32 degrees and very windy. Four thousand five hundred people were watching on that day. The sixth and seventh days were stormy. On the sixth day 9,000 people watched the mountain biking. The seventh day was cooler and 15,000 people watched the marathon. The eighth day was sunny and hot again. Lots of people watched the canoe slalom on the last day.

Day	Temperature	Weather	Sport	Spectators
	30	☀		
			🚲	5,000
	24		🪁	
	27			5,500
			🏄	
	24	🌧		
	22			
	36			6,500

Unit 11   Completing a chart

Composition practice

1 **Use the chart on page 108 to answer these questions about the summer games.**

1 Which sport were people watching on the hottest day and what was the temperature?
   _____ _____

2 Which sport had the most spectators? _____

3 Which sports had the worst weather? _____ _____ _____

4 Which sport were people watching on the coolest day and what was the temperature?
   _____ _____

5 Which sports had the best weather? _____ _____ _____

6 What was the weather like for the wakeboarding? _____

7 Which sport had the fewest spectators? _____

8 What was the weather like for the skateboarding? _____

2 **Write a paragraph about the summer games.**

Use the chart on page 108 for ideas.

You may also look back at exercise 1 on this page for extra ideas.

Before you start writing, think of the best order for the information in the paragraph.

_____
_____
_____
_____
_____
_____
_____
_____
_____

Unit 11 Writing information from a chart

Check-up 11

1 Complete the sentences with one of the words in brackets.

1 Winter is the time _____ people go skiing. (when / which)
2 Football is a sport _____ many people enjoy. (who / that)
3 The Aztecs were people _____ lived in South America. (who / which)
4 This is the cave _____ the treasure was found. (when / where)
5 The first men _____ went to the moon were very brave. (which / that)
6 The film _____ we watched last night was fantastic. (which / who)

2 Change the sentences. Use the relative clauses in the box.
Make sure you put the clauses in the correct place.

> that Henry had taken   who had stolen the jewels   which we gave her
> when people try to escape from the city   where I was born

1 The village has grown into a busy town.
   _____

2 August is a hot month.
   _____

3 Grandma loved the present.
   _____

4 The thief was caught by the police.
   _____

5 The photo won first prize in the competition.
   _____

3 Complete the sentences. Use question tags.

1 You enjoy sport, _____
2 John rides horses, _____
3 We all understand, _____
4 The boys feel tired, _____
5 That dog's noisy, _____
6 I sing badly, _____
7 You all like sweets, _____
8 Your aunt lives in Paris, _____
9 The girls look sad, _____
10 The music sounds lovely, _____

Unit 11   Revision

Check-up 11

Hi, I'm Lily. This is where I always spend my summer holidays.

4 Look.

5 Complete the text. Use the words in the boxes.

| they can lie in the sun and swim   play on the beach every day |
| most people take a holiday   have children   live there |
| she spends at the beach every year   they enjoy the cool, fresh air |
| is on the coast |

that
where
which
who
when

Summer is the time _____.

Some people go to the mountains _____.

Other people, especially those _____, go to a beach _____.

Lily's family always stays in a little town _____.

The people _____ are kind and friendly. Lily is friends with some of the children _____.

Lily loves the three weeks _____.

Unit 11   Revision   **111**

12 Study skills

Learn to correct your own mistakes!

1 There are mistakes in these sentences. Write the sentences correctly.
Remember! v = verb, sp = spelling, w o = word order, a = article

1 (v) (a) My cousins have been to the America two years ago.

2 (w o) (v) Why Linda has cutted her hair?

3 (sp) (v) Listen! The babys cry.

4 (sp) (v) Dad is driveing to work today. He is usually going by bus.

5 (w o) (sp) Never Susie has riden a horse before.

6 (v) (a) (v) (sp) Grandma like flowers and flowers in her garden is beautifull.

2 Find the correct definitions of the underlined words in the box below. Write the numbers.

a Put the top back on the bottle. _____

b The climbers reached the top of the mountain. _____

c Don't stamp on the spider! _____

d Don't forget to put a stamp on the letter. _____

e The farmer put all the sheep in a pen. _____

f You must use a pen in your exams. _____

g You have forgotten to sign your letter. _____

h There was a sign on the gate which said "Keep out!" _____

1	pen n	you use this for writing. It has ink inside.
2	pen n	a small area with a fence around it for keeping animals in
3	sign n	a notice which tells you something
4	sign v	to write your name
5	stamp n	a small piece of paper which you stick on a letter to pay for posting it
6	stamp v	to put your foot down hard on something
7	top n	the summit, the highest point
8	top n	a lid, a cover

Unit 12 Correction techniques; Dictionary skills

Reading comprehension and vocabulary

1 Read *Formula 1!* again.

2 Who said it? Write the name.

 Russ  Tara  Todd  Uncle Pete  Frank Turner

1 The driver is Frank Turner, the national champion. _____
2 These cars go at 220 kilometres an hour! _____
3 I think I'll go and sit in the shade. _____
4 You don't sound very pleased. _____
5 Mum and I are nearly at the track. _____
6 Are you watching the race? _____
7 They've started! _____
8 Who are you? _____
9 It was just like being here. _____
10 I wondered where I had left it. _____

3 Choose the best verb to complete each sentence.

> glance   glare   hesitate   sigh   groan   expect   cheer

1 Everyone _____ when the winning car passed the finishing line.
2 The water in the pool looked cold and Ben _____ before he dived in.
3 Anna only _____ at her book and she didn't read the words properly.
4 Harry _____ the book to be boring and he was surprised because it wasn't.
5 Harry took Ben's pen without asking and Harry _____ at him.
6 The story had a good ending and Lucy _____ happily when she finished it.
7 When Max broke his arm he _____ because of the pain.

Unit 12   Who said it?; cloze

Grammar

1 Match the sentence beginnings and endings.

1. Hurry up! The film is starting
2. I wish
3. After the match had finished,
4. Jenny has been learning French
5. The police caught the thief
6. Lucy wishes
7. The picture will be painted
8. Look! The forest has been destroyed

a the boys went home.
b who had stolen the diamonds.
c she could play the piano.
d in two minutes.
e by fire.
f by a famous artist.
g I had a pet.
h for three years.

1 ___ 2 ___ 3 ___ 4 ___ 5 ___ 6 ___ 7 ___ 8 ___

2 Complete the sentences with the verbs in brackets.

1. Sally wishes she _____ a famous actress. (be)
2. Be quick! The shop _____ soon. (close)
3. Where's the bus? How long _____ we _____ ? (wait)
4. After our visitors _____, we watched TV. (leave)
5. I think next week's match _____ by the Italian team. (win)
6. Grandpa was angry. Someone _____ his window. (break)
7. Look! The plate is empty. All the cakes _____. (eat)
8. Two girls found the money which Grandma _____. (drop)

3 Complete these sentences.

1. I wish I was _____
2. I wish I had _____
3. I wish I could _____

Grammar in conversation.

> Use as many conversational phrases as you can!

1 Your friend is looking fed up. Write your conversation with him/her. You speak first.

What's the matter?

2 You are very happy because something exciting has happened to you. You are talking to a friend. Write the conversation. You speak first.

Hey! Guess what!

Unit 12 Conversation round-up

Spelling

Remember! Some words end in *tion*. These letters sound like *shun*.

fascination

Tara looked at the cars with fascination.

1 Complete the words. Write *-tion*. Read the words.

explana_____   fic_____   stat_____   na_____   opera_____   competi_____

2 Make these verbs into nouns.

Remember! Take the *t* off the verb before you add *tion*.

direct
direction

protect
_____

act
_____

invent
_____

erupt
_____

infect
_____

reflect
_____

3 Use words from this page to complete the sentences.

1 The volcano exploded with a loud _____.
2 Ben saw his _____ in the mirror.
3 The archaeologist gave an interesting _____ of the old ruins.
4 Elbow pads and kneepads give _____ to skateboarders.
5 We met Grandma at the _____.
6 The professor showed us his astonishing new _____.

Unit 12   Spelling: words ending *-tion*

Use of English

Synonyms are words with the same or similar meanings.

Frank Turner was pleased and happy after the race.

1 Read.

1 We can use synonyms to make writing more interesting.

The car looked shiny in the sunshine. The windows shone and the silver wheels were shining, too.

How many times are *shiny* or the verb *to shine* used? _____

Look at these synonyms for shine: sparkle   glitter   Check them in your Dictionary.

Read these sentences with the new words added. Do they make it different? How?

The car looked shiny in the sunlight. The windows sparkled and the silver wheels were glittering, too.

2 We can use synonyms to make a description stronger. Read these two sentences.

There was a little mouse under the flower.

There was a tiny little mouse under the flower.

Which sentence makes the mouse sound smaller? Why?

3 We can use synonyms to give the reader a clearer idea of something.

Inside the cave it was dim and gloomy;
the dark corners were full of black shadows.

What ideas does the sentence give you of the cave?

scary? interesting? dangerous?

The description could be:

Inside the cave it was dim and the corners were dark.

How is this description different to the first one? Does this sentence give you the same ideas?

2 Find synonyms for these words in your Dictionary.

strong   big   interesting   wonderful   afraid

Unit 12   Use of synonyms

Writing preparation

1 Read.

You read the story *Formula 1*. It was told from Russ's point of view.

You wrote the story of the same events. You wrote from Tara's point of view.

2 Think about Todd in the story. Think of answers to these questions.

1 Where was Todd before he spoke to Russ?

What was he thinking and feeling? Write some ideas.

2 Look back at the story. What did Todd do while he was in the car?

Think about the phone conversation from Todd's point of view.

3 What did Russ tell Todd about the race? Write some ideas.

4 What did Todd do when he arrived at the race track? Where did he go? Write notes.

_____

5 Look back at the story. What happened when Todd got to the viewing box?

What did Tara say?   What did Todd say?

Who came into the box? What did he do?

What did everyone say?

Unit 12   Thinking about a point of view

Composition practice

1 Write the story *Formula 1* from Todd's point of view.

Remember to write as if you were Todd. Start like this.

It was the day of Dad's big race and we were stuck in traffic!

Mum said, "I'm sorry Todd. We won't get to the track in time for the start of the race."

I felt very

Check-up 12

1 Complete the sentences with the verbs in brackets.

1 At lunch yesterday Polly _____ the sandwiches which Mum _____ for Alex. (eat, make)
2 Freddy hasn't got a bike. He wishes he _____ one. (have)
3 Where's the bus? How long _____ we _____? (wait)
4 An important visitor _____ to our school next week. (come)
5 I play the piano a little but I wish I _____ it better. (play)
6 Look at the house! All the windows _____. (break)
7 Uncle Jim is working but he wishes he _____ on holiday. (be)
8 After the rain _____, the children _____ outside to play. (stop, go)
9 Next month exams _____ by all the pupils. (take)
10 The children wish they _____ have a party. (can)

2 Complete the sentences with the words in the box.

> Really   What's the matter   That's rubbish   Lucky you

1 Why are you crying? _____?

2 I'm going to the beach this afternoon. _____!

3 There's an elephant in the playground. _____!

4 It's going to snow tomorrow. _____? Are you sure?

Unit 12 Revision

Check-up 12

3 Look at the pictures.

4 Think of a story. Work with a friend if you wish.
Try to include as many of the things in the pictures as you can.

5 Write your story.

_____

6 Give your story a title.

Verb round-up

present continuous with future meaning

Present continuous with future meaning

present perfect and past simple

Portfolio 1: Units 1 and 2

Tick the boxes when you are confident about the task. You can tick in any order.

Grammar

✔ **I can use the present continuous to talk about the future.** ☐

We're going to climb up a volcano tomorrow.

✔ **I can talk about things with *What …!*** ☐

What a fantastic photo!   What an amazing place!
What powerful waves!   What incredible energy!

✔ **I can use reported speech to say what people said.** ☐

He said that he was interested in engines.
She said that she liked science.
They said that they were engineers.
They said that they made turbines.

Reading and understanding

✔ **I have read and understood:**

a diary entry *The land of fire and ice* ☐

information and an explanation of a process *Energy is all around us* ☐

Listening

✔ **I have listened to and understood *Kingfisher Valley*   Part 1 ☐   Part 2 ☐**

Vocabulary

✔ **I know all the key words in: Unit 1 ☐   Unit 2 ☐**

Spelling

✔ **I can read and spell:**

plurals of words ending with *o*:   volcanoes   potatoes   heroes   flamingoes   tomatoes
zoos   cockatoos   kangaroos   hippos   pianos   photos ☐

✔ **I can recognise one- and two-syllable words:**

sea   river   turbine   coast   tower   Earth   steam   mirror   sun   windmill ☐

English World 6 Diploma 1: Units 1 and 2

1 Complete the sentences.

Harry _____ to London next week. (fly)

Use What, What a or What an

_____ ridiculous hat!   _____ clever children!

I am tired.   What did he say?
_____

What did they say?
_____

We play basketball.

2 Answer the questions.

The land of fire and ice What was the guide's name? _____

Energy is all around us What does a generator make? _____

Kingfisher Valley Who lived in Hawkwood House? _____

3 Choose the correct word.

a turbine   a generator   a barrier

A machine that is turned by wind or by liquid is _____.

4 Write the words.

_____ _____ _____ _____

Portfolio 2: Units 3 and 4

Tick the boxes when you are confident about the task. You can tick in any order.

Grammar

✔ I can use the past perfect with *after* and *when*. ☐

After Sam had heard voices, he saw two men on the path.
When Anna had written the letter, she put it in an envelope.

✔ I can use question tags. ☐

This is a beautiful fish, isn't it?
Those lions are sleeping, aren't they?

✔ I can say what one person told another person to do. ☐

The teacher told the children to stop talking.

✔ I can use the present perfect with the past simple. ☐

Have you read this book?
Yes, I have. I read it last week.

Reading and understanding

✔ I have read and understood:

a mystery story *Danger at the old house* ☐

a fable and a poem *The bear and the two travellers; Where is the forest?* ☐

Listening

✔ I have listened to and understood *Kingfisher Valley* Part 3 ☐ Part 4 ☐

Vocabulary ✔ I know all the key words in: Unit 3 ☐ Unit 4 ☐

Spelling ✔ I can read and spell:

words with *dge*: edge badge hedge splodge fridge bridge ☐

words that sound the same but have different spelling and meanings:

poor, paw   right, write   rode, road   some, sum   past, passed   wood, would   wear, where   tied, tide ☐

English World 6 Diploma 2: Units 3 and 4

1 Complete the sentences.

When the children _____ lunch, they _____ out to play. (eat, go)

The bear _____ away after it _____ the man. (go, sniff)

These trees are tall, _____?

This forest is a bit scary, _____?

2 Write what the teachers told or asked the children to do.

Please, open your books.

_____

Finish your work quickly.

_____

3 Answer the questions.

Danger at the old house Who owned the old house? _____

The bear and the two travellers Who pretended to be dead? _____

Where is the forest? What happened to the forest? _____

Kingfisher Valley Who was going to buy the valley? _____

4 Choose the correct word.

   dangerous   very fierce   in danger

An endangered animal is _____.

5 Write the words.

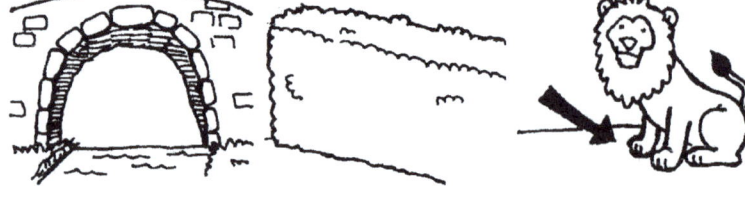

_____ _____ _____ _____

Diploma 2 (Units 3 and 4)

Portfolio 3: Units 5 and 6

Tick the boxes when you are confident about the task. You can tick in any order.

Grammar

✔ I can use the past perfect in a relative clause. ☐

The girl wore the hat that she had made.

✔ I can give my opinion about things. ☐

In my opinion, this is a very good film. I think it's funny.
I disagree. To my mind, it's really silly.

✔ I can use the future passive voice. ☐

Tomorrow the children will be taken to school by car.

✔ I can talk about the present using the present simple and present continuous. ☐

You don't like chocolate, Ben. Why are you eating a chocolate ice cream?

Reading and understanding

✔ I have read and understood:

factual information *The meanings of patterns* ☐

a play *The most amazing fashion show* ☐

Listening

✔ I have listened to and understood *Kingfisher Valley*   Part 5 ☐   Part 6 ☐

Vocabulary

✔ I know all the key words in: Unit 5 ☐   Unit 6 ☐

Spelling

✔ I can read and spell:

words with silent letters inside them: talk walk calf half listen whistle castle ☐

words beginning *re-*: redo refill replace remove rehearse remember replay
repeat repay return ☐

Portfolio 3 (Units 5 and 6)

English World 6 Diploma 3: Units 5 and 6

1 Complete the sentences.

Use the past simple and the past perfect.

Ben _____ the cake that Grandma _____. (like, bake)

The weaver _____ the blanket that he _____. (sell, make)

Use the future passive.

The clothes _____ by the children. (wear)

Use the present simple and the present continuous.

Usually I _____ TV after school but today I'm _____ chess with Sam. (watch, play)

2 Complete the dialogue.

Ben: This game is amazing!

Anna: Yes, I _____. It's fantastic.

Sam: I _____! I _____ it's really boring!

3 Answer the questions.

The meanings of patterns Where do the Quechua people live? _____

The most amazing fashion show Who brought the wrong clothes? _____

Kingfisher Valley Who was Tom Winter? _____

4 Choose the correct word.

closely   confidently   carefully

When you know you can do something well, you do it _____.

5 Write the words.

Don't forget!

Say it again.

Diploma 3 (Units 5 and 6)

Portfolio 4: Units 7 and 8

Tick the boxes when you are confident about the task. You can tick in any order.

Grammar

✔ **I can use indirect pronouns.** ☐

We made Dad a birthday present.

✔ **I can ask for things politely.** ☐

May I have a drink, please?

✔ **I can use the present perfect continuous with *for* and *since*.** ☐

Ben has been jet skiing for half an hour.

Anna has been swimming in the sea since two o'clock.

✔ **I can agree and disagree with other people's opinions.** ☐

I like sailing.   So do I.

I don't like diving.   Neither do I.

Reading and understanding

✔ **I have read and understood:**

a leaflet *An island in the South Pacific* ☐

a legend *How peace came to the people of the great lakes* ☐

Listening

✔ **I have listened to and understood *Adventure in Zarula*** Part 1 ☐ Part 2 ☐

Vocabulary

✔ **I know all the key words in:** Unit 7 ☐   Unit 8 ☐

Spelling

✔ **I can read and spell:**

two-syllable words with a double consonant: parrot rabbit kitten yellow apple hidden swimmer runner coffee foggy lesson pizza ☐

words with *o* sounding *u*: won colour nothing above money month wonderful front love son ☐

English World 6 Diploma 4: Units 7 and 8

1 Complete the sentences.

It was Grandma's birthday so we gave _____ a present.

_____ I borrow your pen, please?

Use the present perfect continuous.

We _____ since this morning. (travel)

Pete _____ his boat for two hours. (sail)

2 Answer the questions.

An island in the South Pacific How was Tahiti formed? _____

How peace came to the people of the great lakes

What was in the hair of the evil chief? _____

Adventure in Zarula Who wanted to steal the diamond? _____

3 Choose the correct word.

   unusual   a stranger   a traveller

A person who is not known by other people is _____.

4 Write the words.

Diploma 4 (Units 7 and 8)

Portfolio 5: Units 9 and 10

Tick the boxes when you are confident about the task. You can tick in any order.

Grammar

✔ **I can use reflexive pronouns.** ☐

Pete fell down and hurt himself badly.

✔ **I can use the past continuous and past simple with *when*.** ☐

When we were walking to school, an ambulance went past very fast.

✔ **I can use the present perfect passive.** ☐

Hospitals have been built all over the world.

✔ **I can wish for things.** ☐

I wish I had a car and I wish I could drive.

Reading and understanding

✔ **I have read and understood:**

information and instructions *The first doctors* ☐

information and a description of a process *Plants in medicine* ☐

Listening

✔ **I have listened to and understood *Adventure in Zarula*** Part 3 ☐ Part 4 ☐

Vocabulary

✔ **I know all the key words in:** Unit 9 ☐ Unit 10 ☐

Spelling

✔ **I can read and spell:**

three-syllable words: microscope medicine hospital important instruction ☐

words beginning or ending with *al*: almost alright altogether also always already

several medical festival material hospital ☐

English World 6 Diploma 5: Units 9 and 10

1 Complete the sentences.

I've hurt _____ on this sharp thorn.

The doctor _____ to the nurse when the phone _____. (talk, ring)

People _____ by doctors for thousands of years. (help)

Ben _____ that he _____ a new computer. (wish, have)

2 Answer the questions.

The first doctors Which country did Imhotep work in? _____

Plants in medicine Where does the rosy periwinkle grow? _____

Adventure in Zarula How did the friends escape from the island? _____

3 Choose the correct word.

anxious   dangerous   infectious

A person who worries a lot is _____.

4 Write the words.

_____   _____

This word means *nearly*.

_____   _____

Diploma 5 (Units 9 and 10)

Portfolio 6: Units 11 and 12

Tick the boxes when you are confident about the task. You can tick in any order.

Grammar

✔ **I can use relative clauses with *who*, *which*, *that*, *when*, *where*.** ☐

Twelve o'clock is the time when the race will start.

There is the man who won the race.

The boat which came first had a blue sail.

The place where the race ended is behind the trees.

✔ **I can use question tags with *do*.** ☐

Racing cars go very fast, don't they?

Your dad drives fast, doesn't he?

You like racing, don't you?

Reading and understanding

✔ **I have read and understood:**

information and information in a chart *Extreme sports!* ☐

a story from a point of view *Formula 1!* ☐

Listening

✔ **I have listened to and understood *Adventure in Zarula*** Part 5 ☐ Part 6 ☐

Vocabulary

✔ **I know all the key words in:** Unit 11 ☐ Unit 12 ☐

Spelling

✔ **I can read and spell:**

words ending -*or*: actor doctor professor author sailor inventor
visitor mayor tailor editor ☐

words ending -*tion*: station nation fiction competition operation
explanation fascination ☐

English World 6 Diploma 6: Units 11 and 12

1 Complete the sentences.

This is the place _____ the car stopped.

This is the time _____ you should do your homework.

He is the skier _____ won the gold cup.

There is the car _____ my dad drives.

You like skiing, _____?

Anna watches sports, _____?

2 Answer the questions.

Extreme sports! Which sport needs a kite? _____

Formula 1! Who did Russ talk to on the phone? _____

Adventure in Zarula Where was the real diamond? _____

3 Choose the correct word.

   hestitate   shuffle   desperate

If you stop for a moment before you do something you _____.

4 Write the words.

_____   _____

_____   _____

Diploma 6 (Units 11 and 12)

Vocabulary

For every unit, learn lists 1 and 2. Make sure you understand what the words mean. Check in your dictionary if you are not sure.
Try to learn the other lists in each unit, too.

Unit 1

List 1 (10)

active
fountain
mud
peculiar
spectacular
tap (plumbing)
terrifying
thrilling
volcano
weird

List 2 (10)

bubble v
crater
dangerous
diary
dragon
erupt
eruption
guide
rough
student

List 3 (9)

bet v
feed
hot spring
Iceland
lava
personal
point (of view)
steam v
tomato

List 4 (9)

expert
geologist
geyser
glacier
kingfisher
lynx
rare
shoot up (go up fast)
wildlife

Unit 2

List 1 (10)

barrier
blade
calculator
discuss
explanation
face v
natural
renewable
run out (end)
windmill

List 2 (10)

amount
battery
coast
energy
material
power v n
reflect
steam n
tide
turbine

List 3 (9)

decision
generator
look (appearance) n
puzzled
secret
solar cells
spare
    spare time
trust v
waterwheel

Unit 3

List 1 (10)

bank (river) n
binoculars
flow
gap
imagine
lock v
promise
rusty
single
underneath

List 2 (10)

bump into
dead
dull
event
expect
fact
    in fact
iron (metal)
mysterious
mystery
season

List 3 (9)

board up
nail v
peer
relief
rod (fishing)
shudder v
sigh v
trapped adj
weed n

List 4 (9)

belong
borrow
briefcase
fuss n
gasp n
padlock
set up v
temper
upstream

Unit 4

List 1 (10)

bear
cry (call out)
destroy
endangered
fearless
file (fact file)
panda
pretend
repeat
rhyme

List 2 (10)

advice
cattle
chorus
fable
fellow
fortunately
habitat
pitch (football)
safety
timid

List 3 (9)

about
kangaroo
koala bear
moral
rhythm
risk
    at risk
sniff
sweet adj
verse

Unit 5

List 1 (10)

ancient
apron
blouse
countryside
cruel
headscarf
paragraph
title
traditional
village

List 2 (10)
altogether
apart
blackberry
exactly
freedom
heading
hollow *adj*
information
Ireland
meaning

List 3 (10)
brain
complete
leave alone
love
react
rubbish
skill
strength
waste
    waste of time
zoo

List 4 (10)
century
complicated
crop
motherhood
plain
pullover
represent
sub-heading
tray
TV station

Unit 6

List 1 (10)
airport
breathlessly
business trip
confidently
designer
    sunglasses
fancy dress
fashion
    fashion show
sort out
stage directions

List 2 (7)
cotton
fluffy
gorgeous
Malaysia
Scottish
shy
silky

List 3 (7)
comic
match *v*
nephews
nieces
patterned
plot
project

Unit 7

List 1 (10)
activity
attractive
calm
canoe
encourage
hidden
jet-ski
meet
sparkling
windsurf

List 2 (9)
arrange
clear
effect
explore
horseback
lagoon
persuade
reef
wise

List 3 (8)
cute
lend
magic
pathway
South Pacific
surf
turquoise
volcanic

Unit 8

List 1 (10)
arrival
chief
fear
gentle
hate
heart
kindly
native *adj*
warrior
wisely

List 2 (10)
cause
harm
law
legend
meanwhile
neighbour
opposite
peace
sadness
ugliness

List 3 (8)
meeting
mind
    don't mind
nation
part (role)
spread *v*
stranger
tribe
truth
    tell the truth

List 4 (7)
arrow
bow
bury
hideous
horror
paddle (canoe) *v*
weapons

Unit 9

List 1 (10)
ambulance
drain
factual
health
healthy
illness
instructions
medicine (field)
properly
sheets (bed)

List 2 (10)
divide
European
fresh
microscope
Middle East
obvious
operation
pain
treat (medicine)
treatment

Vocabulary

List 3 (9)
cleanliness
disgrace
disposable
instruments
pharaoh
surgeon
touch *n*
ward
wrong
   go wrong

Unit 10

List 1 (10)
anxious
blood
bone
cure
fever
life
   life cycle
serious
sore
tablet
throat

List 2 (10)
bark
bud
clearing
crack *v*
petals
process
root
shoot (of plant)
stem
trunk (of tree)

List 3 (7)
calm *v*
fed up
hate *v*
normally
painkiller
recently
unfold

List 4 (6)
daylight
forever
light *v*
passage
   secret passage
raft
torch

Unit 11

List 1 (10)
compete
competition
competitor
elbow
   elbow pad
height
kite
   kite surfer
   kite surfing
protective
rough (water)
speed *n v*
take place

List 2 (10)
chart
equipment
knee
   kneepad
life-jacket
Olympic
ramp
spectator
steep
   steeply
tie
twist

List 3 (10)
BMX biker
   BMX biking
canoeing
downhill
extreme
freestyle
goggles
in-line skates
   in-line skating
puzzle
skis
slalom

List 4 (11)
biking
control *v*
fool
marathon
mountain biker
   mountain
   biking
pole
skateboard
   skateboarder
   skateboarding
snowboarder
   snowboarding
wake
   wakeboarder
   wakeboarding
whizz *v*

Unit 12

List 1 (10)
astonished
bee
chat
cheer
cheerio
commentator
desperate
hesitate
shade
suppose

List 2 (10)
bench
champion
dim
expect
fascination
gasp
groan
hug
sigh
upstairs

List 3 (7)
beam
glare
miss (not see) *v*
over (finished) *v*
shuffle
turn away
viewing box

List 4 (6)
burst
chequered
grandstand
run (engine)
surge
turn back

Vocabulary

Macmillan Education Limited
4 Crinan Street
London N1 9XW

Companies and representatives throughout the world

ISBN 978-0-230-02482-3

Text © Mary Bowen and Liz Hocking 2010
Design and illustration © Macmillan Education Limited 2010

The authors have asserted their rights to be identified as the authors of this work in accordance with the Copyright, Designs and Patents Act 1988.

First published 2010

All rights reserved; no part of this publication may be
reproduced, stored in a retrieval system, transmitted in any
form, or by any means, electronic, mechanical, photocopying,
recording, or otherwise, without the prior written permission
of the publishers.

Original design by Anthony Godber
Illustrated by Juliet Breese and Chantel Kees
Cover design by Andrew Oliver
Page make-up by Wild Apple Design

The publishers would like to thank the following for their participation in the development of this course:
In Egypt – Inas Agiz, Salma Ahmed, Hekmat Aly, Suzi Balaban, Mohamed Eid, Bronwen El Kholy, Mostafa El Makhzangy, Hala Fouad, Jonathan French, Nashaat Nageeb Gendy, Hisham Howeedy, Saber Lamey, Heidi Omara, Maha Radwan, Amany Shawkey, Christine Abu Sitta, Ali Abdel Wahab
In Russia – Tatiana Antonova, Elena Belonozhkina, Galina Dragunova, Irina Filonenko, Marina Gaisina, Maria Goretaya, Oksana Guzhnovskaya, Irina Kalinina, Olga Kligerman, Galina Kornikova, Lidia Kosterina, Sergey Kozlov, Irina Larionova, Irina Lenchenko, Irina Lyubimova, Karine Makhmuryan, Maria Pankina, Anna Petrenkova, Elena Plisko, Natalia Vashchenko, Angelika Vladyko

Printed and bound in Poland by CGS

2025 2024 2023 2022 2021
43 42 41 40 39 38 37 36 35 34

 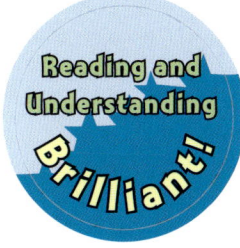 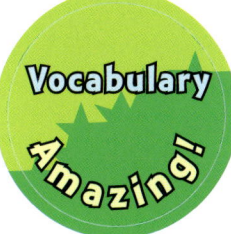  

 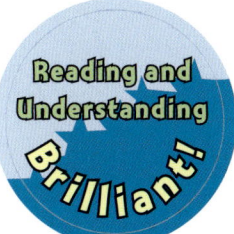 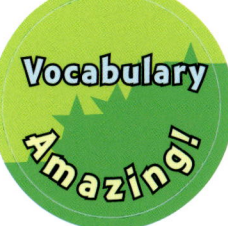  

 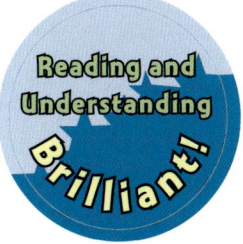 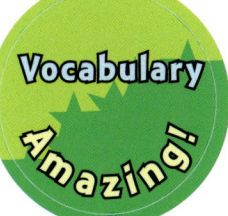  

  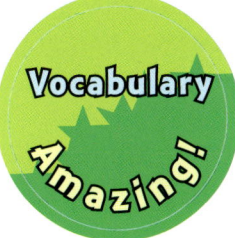  

 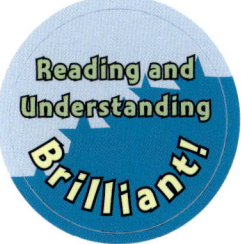 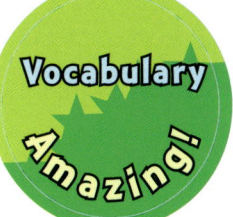